D0984928

Walter Holtkamp

American Organ Builder

Walter Holtkamp
American Organ Builder
John Allen Ferguson

THE KENT STATE UNIVERSITY PRESS

Copyright© 1979 by The Kent State University Press,
Kent, Ohio 44242

All rights reserved
Library of Congress Catalog Card Number: 78–26500
ISBN: 0–87338–217–X
Manufactured in the United States of America

Library of Congress Cataloging in Publication Data

Ferguson, John Allen, 1941-
  Walter Holtkamp, American organ builder.

  Bibliography: p.
  1. Holtkamp, Walter, 1894–1962. 2. Organ-builders—
United States—Biography. 3. Organs—United States.
ML424.H77F5   786.6'22'4 [B]   78–26500
ISBN 0–87338–217–X

Contents

Foreword by Arthur Poister   viii
Preface   x
Acknowledgments   xii

1. Walter Holtkamp (1894-1962)   1
2. Years of Transition (1931-1933)   17
3. Radical Years (1933-1945)   24
4. Towards a Mature Style (1945-1950)   49
5. Mature Years (1950-1962)   63
6. The Visual Dimension   75
7. Epilog   85
Notes   90

Appendix A: *Stoplists of Significant Instruments
Discussed in the Text*   96
   I. Detroit Society of the New Church, Detroit, Michi-
      gan
  II. All Saints Episcopal Church, Minot, North Dakota
 III. Brunnerdale Seminary, Canton, Ohio
  IV. St. John's Lutheran Church, Cleveland, Ohio
   V. Cleveland Museum of Art, Cleveland, Ohio
  VI. St. John's Roman Catholic Church, Covington,
      Kentucky
 VII. Miles Park Presbyterian Church, Cleveland,
      Ohio

VIII. St. James' Episcopal Church, Cleveland Ohio

IX. Emmanuel Lutheran Church, Rochester, New York

X. Baldwin-Wallace College, Berea, Ohio

XI. Our Lady of the Angels Roman Catholic Church, Cleveland, Ohio

XII. Draft Stoplist, a Minimum Organ

XIII. First Unitarian Church, Cleveland, Ohio

XIV. Cleveland Museum of Art, Cleveland, Ohio

XV. St. Paul's Lutheran Church, Cleveland, Ohio

XVI. Practice Organ—Oberlin College, Oberlin, Ohio

XVII. Syracuse University—Crouse Hall, Syracuse, New York

XVIII. Yale University, Battell Chapel, New Haven, Connecticut

XIX. St. Paul's Episcopal Church, Cleveland, Ohio

XX. Massachusetts Institute of Technology Chapel, Cambridge, Massachusetts

XXI. St. John's Abbey, Collegeville, Minnesota

Appendix B: *Chronological List of Instruments by Walter Holtkamp* 130

Contents

List of Illustrations

Walter Holtkamp at Work   *frontispiece*
The Cleveland Museum of Art Rückpositiv and the
    experimental organ (later installed in Our Lady of
    Peace Church, Cleveland) erected in the factory   16
The Cleveland Museum of Art, 1933   21
Detail of the Rückpositiv   26
St. John's Church, Covington, Kentucky, erected in
    the factory   29
Miles Park Presbyterian Church, Cleveland   33
The Portativ   35
Baldwin-Wallace College, Berea, Ohio   40
Fairmount Presbyterian Church, Cleveland,
    Rückpositiv   42
Cleveland Museum of Art, 1946   48
Walter Holtkamp with Albert Schweitzer at the Cleve-
    land Museum of Art   51
Crouse Hall, Syracuse University   55
St. Paul's Lutheran Church, Cleveland   56
Walter Holtkamp with Arthur Poister at the first "Mar-
    tini" for Syracuse University   59
Battell Chapel, Yale University   62
St. Paul's Episcopal Church, Cleveland   64
Walter Holtkamp with André Marchal at the Mas-
    sachusetts Institute of Technology   72
Massachusetts Institute of Technology Chapel, Cam-
    bridge, Massachsetts   77
The Holtkamp Console   79
Concordia Seminary, St. Louis, Missouri   83
Walter Holtkamp at the experimental organ   87

Sources Cited   141

Foreword

The twentieth century renaissance in organ building has been of continuing great interest to organists, builders, and enthusiasts, and much has been studied, discussed and written about it. However, attention in a popular movement is often focused mainly on one facet of the movement, thus tending to minimize or overlook another equally important aspect. Such is the case in regard to Walter Holtkamp and his work. This study addresses that situation by bringing the complete story of his important work before the organ world. Here was a man of rare integrity and idealism who refused to compromise his artistic principles. A pioneer in the reform movement from almost the beginning of his career, he has long been a legendary figure in the organ world. This study provides the real story of the man and his work, thus giving background, substance and direction to the legend.

As a friend, colleague and admirer of Walter Holtkamp and his work I am most happy that this book has at long last come into being. It will be of tremendous value to the organ world not only for the historic record it so interestingly traces, but for bringing out Walter Holtkamp's unique contribution to the development of the American organ and for placing him in the record as one of the outstanding builders of the first half of the twentieth century.

Arthur Poister
Syracuse University

Preface

Early in the twentieth century, certain German organists and scholars began to question the artistic merit of most modern organs. Along with other developments, the rediscovery of the Schnitger organ in St. Jacobi, Hamburg, and the construction in 1921 of an instrument for the University of Freiburg using a disposition conceived by Praetorius in 1618 turned the attention of organists to the work that had been done in the past. The concerts and conferences stimulated by these two instruments inspired a revival of interest in the art of organ building as it had been practiced in earlier centuries.

Before long, news of these European developments reached America, and by 1930 an American organ revival had begun. Among those Americans involved in the revival, the name of Walter Holtkamp (1894–1962) stands out. Many authorities credit him with being the first American organ builder to adopt the principles of the renaissance in organ building that had already started in Europe. Today his name is synonymous with a certain style of American organ building, much as the name of Schnitger is synonymous with a certain style of European organ building.

This book, the first major work to study the art of Walter Holtkamp, has a twofold purpose: first, to gain some understanding of the ideals that motivated Holtkamp's development of his unique style of organ building, and second, to trace the development of that style by an examination of instruments, as well as designs for instruments, from each of the periods of his career. Such an examination, especially of the earlier instruments, is of interest because, although most organists are familiar with the mature Holtkamp instruments, many are not aware of the remarkable nature of much of his early work.

In preparing this book, I have relied on three major sources: factory records and extensive conversations with Walter Holtkamp, Jr.; conversations and correspondence with the friends and colleagues of Walter Holtkamp, Sr.; and examination of the instruments themselves. Fortunately, most of the early Holtkamp organs have not been replaced or rebuilt, and since the Holtkamp business was primarily regional until after World War II, most of the earlier organs are in northeastern Ohio, allowing me the opportunity to see, hear, and play most of them personally.

This study has convinced me that Holtkamp was the most radical of the early American converts to reform in organ building. Most of the important firsts in this country, from the Rückpositiv to mechanical action, can be documented as being his work. But in introducing these principles of design, developed centuries earlier in Europe, Holtkamp was not interested in building copies. He was interested in building a truly unique American organ, designed for the physical environments encountered in this country, as well as for the more eclectic demands made upon American organs. As Holtkamp makes clear in his writings and speeches, he saw himself as an American whose work was leavened, but not limited, by European examples. His reputation and unique position among American organ builders are testimony to his success.

Acknowledgements

I am grateful for the willing assistance of the many people who so graciously shared their insights into the life and work of Walter Holtkamp. Special mention should be made of Arthur Poister and Russell Saunders, whose encouragement and interest helped to get this project launched. Dr. M. Alfred Bichsel gave enthusiastic assistance in reading and reacting to this project in its first form as a doctoral dissertation at the Eastman School of Music. In preparation for publication, Michael Di Battista of the Kent State University Press provided wise editorial counsel while Phyllis Gordon's quick eye for detail provided a final check for accuracy as she typed the final draft.

A very special debt is owed to Walter Holtkamp, Jr., who spent many hours with me and assisted in locating material and information essential to a responsible study of the subject. The factory archives and library were placed at my disposal, and no attempts were made to color or influence my conclusions. Thus, although this study would have been impossible without the complete cooperation of Walter Holtkamp, Jr., the material presented and conclusions reached remain solely my responsibility.

Finally, the encouragement and patience of my wife, Ruth, has provided a reservoir of support much needed and deeply appreciated.

Walter Holtkamp
American Organ Builder

1
Walter Holtkamp
(1894-1962)

In the year 1858 Herman Heinrich Holtkamp was born in New Knoxville, Ohio. Holtkamp the first, who liked to be called Henry, was the son of a German immigrant and grew up on his father's small farm in New Knoxville, a small town in west central Ohio. There he met, and in 1881 married, Sophia Elizabeth Schroer, member of another German family in the town. This strong German background, with its heritage of interest in the arts, revealed itself in Henry Holtkamp, who became interested in music and learned to play the piano and organ. His abilities must have delighted his father, who encouraged all his children to develop their musical abilities and gave each of his six eldest children a piano or organ. Eventually Henry's interest and abilities in music, together with a remarkable natural gift of salesmanship, led him to move his wife and family to the nearby larger town of St. Mary's where, in the early 1890s, he established a music store, selling pianos, harmoniums, and an occasional organ. For the organs he usually dealt with the Cleveland firm of G. F. Votteler and Co.; through this association, and because of his marked ability as a salesman, he was invited in 1903 to move to Cleveland and assume responsibility for the firm's sales.[1]

One of many small, regional organ builders in the United States at the turn of the century, Votteler was founded in

1855 by Gottlieb F. Votteler, a German who immigrated in 1847 (coincidentally the same year as Walter Holtkamp's grandfather came to America). When Henry Holtkamp moved to Cleveland in 1903, Votteler and Company was already 50 years old and under the control of Henry B. Votteler, son of the founder, Gottlieb Votteler, who had died in 1894. The firm was first located on West Third Street north of Rockwell Avenue, and then moved south on West Third to a location across from the building housing the German language newspaper, a site presently under Cleveland's Terminal Tower. The business was then relocated at West Fourteenth and Abbey Streets, its location at the time the Holtkamp family joined the firm. In 1922 the company moved to a new building at 2909 Meyer Avenue and has remained in this location to date.[2]

The minutes of a directors' meeting dated 15 September 1903 list Henry Holtkamp as an officer of the company. The same minutes also record a change of name from G. F. Votteler to Votteler-Hettche, reflecting the contribution of capital by another new partner, John Hettche, owner of a local brewery. In 1905 Henry Votteler retired and Hettche lost interest in the busines, leaving control of the company in the hands of Henry Holtkamp. In 1911 Allen Gordon Sparling joined the firm to take charge of the shop. He was a mechanical expert with little interest in tonal matters, leaving such considerations to Henry Holtkamp, who served as salesman and public figure for the firm (a tradition continued by Walter, Sr., and Walter, Jr.). In 1914 the articles of incorporation were changed from their 1903 version to Votteler-Holtkamp-Sparling Organ Co., reflecting the new organization and ownership of the firm. In 1951 the name was changed to Holtkamp Organ Company, reflecting the present ownership of the firm, now exclusively a family business.

The arrival of Henry Holtkamp and Allen Gordon Sparling had a positive influence on the fortunes of the firm and the average yearly production of instruments more than doubled from six in the years 1903–09 to 14 for the years 1910–19. Through the 1920s the firm continued to prosper, and deliver as many as 23 organs in a single year (1928). This continued prosperity is also noteworthy in that the smaller, regionally based organ companies were having a difficult time competing with the emerging large and influential builders like Austin, Möller and Skinner.[3]

The instruments constructed by Votteler-Holtkamp-Sparling were more conservative than those made by the new giants in the industry. Votteler-Holtkamp-Sparling continued to utilize mechanical action into the second decade of the twentieth century. Since most of their instruments were relatively small, the "advantages" of the new electric action in ease of control over a large instrument were not so important. It is difficult to be too innovative in a more modest organ, and Votteler-Holtkamp-Sparling had neither the reputation nor the facilities to attract contracts for the huge orchestral organs being built by the larger companies, although they did produce a few theatre organs and experiment with player mechanisms. The influences of the age did have their effect upon the organs of Votteler-Holtkamp-Sparling as wind pressures were increased, more unison registers specified, and console gadgets introduced. Some stoplists even abandoned traditional nomenclature and utilized simple orchestral names, as the Aeolian Company often did in their residence organs (String F, String P, Horn F, etc.).

One tonal innovation of the firm from this period, the unique Ludwigtone, deserves mention. Named for an old monk known as Brother Ludwig, the register was considered perfect for the accompaniment of chant, and became a

3

standard feature on even the smallest of Votteler-Holt-kamp-Sparling organs. Walter Holtkamp continued to utilize this register until about 1940. The stop, an open flue register made of wood, resembles a Dopple Flute in that it has two mouths. The pipes are of slender scale, but with unusual depth to allow for a center partition, which provides two vibrating columns of air. They are voiced as a gentle flute and tuned, one side flat and the other sharp of unison, to yield a refined celeste with a slow roll to the tone. William Barnes considers its sound to be "somewhat more mysterious than that produced by two separate ranks of pipes."[4] It is perhaps appropriate that the single tonal innovation claimed by the small builders Votteler-Holtkamp-Sparling should be the gentle Ludwigtone rather than the Tuba Mirabilis claimed by the giant Ernest Skinner.[5]

Thus it was in the environment of a small and modest family business that Walter Holtkamp's understanding of the organ, its literature, and the art of organ building was first shaped. Born in St. Mary's on 1 July 1894, the fifth of six children, the young boy moved to Cleveland with his family when his father joined the Votteler firm in 1903. Walter Holtkamp attended the public schools in Cleveland and Lakewood, dropping out of high school to seek his fortune as a crew member on the Great Lakes ore carriers. While he had worked intermittently in his father's shop from the age of fourteen, and his early journals show him on the road for the firm as early as 1913, he did not want to be an organ builder and never formally studied organ building. His lack of commitment to organ building notwithstanding, he worked regularly in the shop from 1916 until he enlisted in the United States Army in June 1917. His service in the army during World War I included almost a year of duty in France from June 1918 to March 1919. His European service provided him an opportunity to listen to and study many organs, especially in France where he was stationed, but he was not interested. He could have remained in Europe after the war for travel and study, but his lack of interest in organ building discouraged any serious work or study during this European sojourn.[6]

Yet, upon his discharge in 1919, he returned to the firm, fast becoming a family business since his elder sister Mary Holtkamp had already joined the firm as well. Walter Holtkamp spent much of his time on the road and made frequent trips to Minnesota, even speculating on moving there to seek his fortune. But in the early 1920s he decided to remain in the business, joined the Lakewood Country Club, and set about establishing himself in the community as a suburban businessman. Also during the 1920s, he met Margaret McClure of Lakewood, married her on 5 January 1928, and adopted Mary and David, her children by a previous marriage. Their son, Walter, Jr., was born on 20 March 1929.

Walter Holtkamp's first decade of serious organ building coincided with the end of what is now considered to be the darkest period in the history of American organ building. The popularity of the theatre organ and the mechanical flexibility of the perfected electric actions conspired to encourage organ builders in all the wrong directions. The goal was to make an instrument of great variety and power. Tonally, the unison register of great character and individuality, and thus little potential for ensemble blend, reigned supreme.

Organ building also shared an interest in the large, the complex and the colossal that was so much a part of the American life style of the times. Electricity allowed for the placement of the pipes almost anywhere—in the attic, the basement, and sometimes a former closet. Orpha Ochse sums up the state of affairs most succinctly when she writes, "One wonders if an organ contract was ever turned down in this period because the organ would have to be placed in an unfortunate location."[7]

Much insight into Walter Holtkamp's development as an organ builder is provided by a fascinating sketch that I discovered in the company archives. The sketch was written by Joseph Sittler, Professor Emeritus of the University of Chicago Divinity School, who served Cleveland's Messiah Lutheran Church from 1930 to 1943, and watched with interest Holtkamp's development during this critical period in his career. The sketch, written during Sittler's Cleveland ministry, begins with perceptive comments on Holtkamp's reactions to American organ building as it was practiced during his first decade of serious organ building.

> During the period of his apprenticeship Holtkamp, like most people of the period, was intrigued by the modern electro-pneumatic organ mechanisms. He shared the typical American fascination for gadgets, for and by themselves, and for their possibilities. Tone became subservient to mechanism. Excellence became a mechanical term in a tonal aspiration. He shared the typical fondness for the unusual tone. Luscious tone quality, the aspiration of the period, was implemented by the ease of these gadgets. On the organs of the time a boom or a whisper were both mechanically available. What the organ of this type did with the music was a secondary consideration. Celerity and wide flexibility of tonal possibilities were the first things to be sought.[8]

Holtkamp's apprenticeship came to an abrupt end in the spring of 1931. Henry Holtkamp was taken ill in Minot, North Dakota, while on a business trip. His illness proved fatal and he never returned to Cleveland, remaining in St. Joseph's Hospital in Minot until his death on 16 March 1931. Just three months later, Mary Holtkamp was injured in an automobile accident while on company business. Her injuries proved fatal, and with her death on 20 June 1931,

Walter Holtkamp found himself in control of the artistic direction of the firm. With Allen Sparling as the only other principal in the business and America in the midst of its worst depression, it was not an encouraging time to assume such responsibility.

"The Walter Holtkamp of the year 1931 was a tall, very slender, softly-speaking man of 36, of a studious mien, who liked to sit at his desk with a copy of Albert Schweitzer's *Out of My Life and Thought* before him."[9] This description of Walter Holtkamp gives us an accurate if somewhat romanticized picture of a man who, in the dark days of the Depression, was most happy when talking about organ music and organ building with his organist friends, and when working with his men in the factory. A feeling of trust, almost a partnership between the men and their boss, quickly evolved in the shop on Meyer Avenue. Even in his later days, Holtkamp was ready to help with the work if needed, and Grigg Fountain remembers seeing him on the job soldering wires.[10] Holtkamp was not himself a voicer, although he had tried his hand at this, as well as all other phases of organ building, during his apprenticeship, and relied upon his talented voicers to execute his wishes. Together they developed their own jargon (too edgy, too fluty, etc.) for the discussion of tonal characteristics, and the voicers were dependent upon Holtkamp for direction in producing the desired results. He spent much time in the voicing rooms, perhaps more than many builders, to evolve the sounds he had in mind. While he did deal with matters of pipe scaling in the design of his instruments, his work was always more subjective than objective, and often his specifications were not too specific about scaling details and would express the design of a new instrument in relation to other jobs already constructed.[11]

In addition to the close work with his men in the shop, the continuing association with organists and musicians sympathetic to his ideas was of central importance to the development of his work. Members of the Cleveland American Guild of Organists Chapter were regular visitors to the shop in the early 1930s, with one meeting a year in the shop. Often Holtkamp would address the group, which provided him a cross-section of organists upon whom he could try out his evolving ideas. One year he hosted G. Donald Harrison, who spoke on his approach to organ building. But usually the gatherings involved music making on an instrument set up in the erecting room. In 1934 a most remarkable concert was held in the shop for the AGO, featuring, among others, Walter Blodgett and Robert Noehren performing on both organ (the Covington, Kentucky, instrument) and Challis harpsichords provided by John Challis, who had been visiting the factory for a week of music making and experimentation with organ, harpsichord, and clavichord. The program was quite extensive and ambitious, including even a Bach Brandenburg Concerto.

Yet these large-scale encounters with musicians, significant as they were, cannot compare to the impact that the dialog with certain individuals, especially those organists closest to him, had upon Holtkamp. In this regard John Fesperman clearly articulates the importance of the rediscovery of the organist by the organ builder and vice versa. Together they looked anew at the literature for their instrument, which then informed their thoughts on organ building.

> The central musical fact, rediscovered between roughly 1930 and 1960, was that the organ could be fully understood only in relation to its repertoire. The renaissance which has taken place is essentially a musical one, and the thread which binds it together is the collaboration

between musicians and organ builders. It took both Walter Holtkamp *and* Melville Smith, for instance, to produce the 1933 Positiv in the Cleveland Museum.[12]

Holtkamp, probably more than any other American organ builder of his time, actively sought out organists, some of whom became important influences upon his work. The literature for the instrument was another important influence. The texts of every talk Holtkamp gave about his art mention the organ literature, and especially the music of Bach, as the supreme test of an organ's efficacy.

Early in his career, Holtkamp enjoyed writing and speaking about his work, although at that point his work was not well known and he had few prestigous contracts. Thus his articles and speeches provided a good means of presenting himself to potential clients. At this time, as Phelps makes clear, he enjoyed the role of radical.[13] His most outspoken comments usually related to his concern for bringing the instrument into the room in which it was to sound.

> When the various divisions of an organ are all placed in the open—that is within the four walls, ceiling and floor of an auditorium, this auditorium acts as a chamber and qualifies the tone of all. *But* the audience is also in the auditorium, that is, within the same chamber, so it doesn't matter. The theory of the mixing chamber for the organ and choir is a mystery to me. I cannot understand it. Nor can I believe that such a phenomenon is desirable, even if it does occur. To my ears, chambers and/or chancels are qualifiers, not mixers. I don't want my tone mixed, predigested and rendered into any impersonal mass. I prefer to sit in the same room with the pipes and do my own mixing.[14]

Writing for the journal *Architecture*, he put his ideas in a different, more humorous, but equally firm way.

> The world of music would be everlastingly indebted to the architect who would bring the organ out into the open and insist that it be treated so as to provide the organist an opportunity to comprehend the

nature of his medium. The artist-musician, whether he plays a kettle-drum or a violin, is sensitive to his instrument and merges himself physically with it. With present conditions of organ placement, the organist is in the unfortunate position of the man who must woo his lady by correspondence.[15]

The reputation of the blunt crusader generated by these talks and articles not only didn't hurt his business, but fit well with his basic personality.

The stories of Walter Holtkamp and his personality are many: he is a legend. While recollections differ, all agree that Walter Holtkamp was a strong-willed man; he was, in fact, downright stubborn. He often seemed to enjoy being difficult, especially with potential clients who were unknown to him. He was famous for his acid comments to ministers and organ committee members who questioned his ideas about the importance of an open placement of his instruments, often while the organists involved stood helplessly by, thinking all hope for a new instrument doomed in the argument. Such tales document Holtkamp's desire to test clients' commitment to his concepts of organ building. Often negotiations would progress to a seeming impasse and Holtkamp would refuse to compromise and threaten not to build the organ unless he could get his way. Such courage and conviction remain somewhat the exception for American organ builders. In this regard, organ builder Charles McManis observes, "Architects found him adamant in his demands for placement of his instruments. Not all of us have been able to be that rigid."[16]

Yet once convinced of a person's interest in his work, Holtkamp would bend a bit and could even be quite patient when he wanted to be, as Arthur Poister points out in the following anecdote:

Well, speaking of trying out ideas, and bullheadedness, and Walter was bullheaded we'll agree . . . Syracuse University was awfully good to me. In addition to the Crouse organ, a renovation of the chapel organ was planned. When Walter came, Harrison had already agreed to do a patch-up job but Walter said no it must be from scratch. When we talked about the design of the chapel organ I said, "Walter, you'll be disappointed in me." This was before Crouse was installed. For the chapel I wanted Swell, Great and enclosed Choir. Well, he tried to talk me into an unenclosed Positiv. Finally he said, "We'll wait and see." Then Crouse was in and after a few months I said, "What am I crabbing about a Choir. I'd rather have a Positiv that has some guts or *stug* instead of a clarinet and an Unda Maris." Next time Walter came, I had been quite adamant and wondered how I was going to let him know of my change in thinking. I told him that I'd come to the conclusion Hendricks should be a Positiv instead of a Choir. "Ha," he said and laughed and slapped the seat. But he had been willing to wait for me to come 'round. So he did have patience, he was firm in his thinking but when it came to talking with someone who had ideas basically like himself, he was willing to play around long enough for that someone to catch up with him.[17]

As Holtkamp's fame as a designer spread he often was called upon to submit a design for an organ. To him, such a request required more than a proposed stoplist and price tag. The request would precipitate a design study, often so thorough that it included the preparation of a scale model of the room with the instrument placed in it. Such a process was expensive and time-consuming, and Holtkamp soon discovered that some clients were not serious enough to justify such an investment of time and energy. Accordingly he established a procedure whereby the clients signed a retainer agreement engaging him to work with the client's representatives to decide upon an effective and proper location for the organ and to prepare a design, architectural and tonal, for the organ. The fee, substantial enough to assure that the client was in earnest, was subtracted from the contract price of the instrument if eventually con-structed, or the client could take the resulting design to other builders for bids. Perhaps the most famous design executed by another builder is the Air Force Academy organ.

Many stories are told about Holtkamp's visiting institutions for a design consultation. One such tale again demonstrates his concern for the placement of his instruments, while at the same time revealing a shrewd judge of human nature at work. Holtkamp was invited to visit a newly completed church, the organ committee of which proposed placing the organ in large chambers on both sides of the rear gallery. Holtkamp's reaction was to say that one-half of the proposed organ budget, invested in an instrument free-standing across the rear of the gallery, would be twice as effective as the entire budget wasted by placing the organ in the tombs provided by the architect. Some of the committee were not convinced, and Holtkamp proposed attending Sunday worship to "test the acoustics when filled" to see if he was correct in his judgments. He appeared the next day wearing the traditional beret and carrying a camp stool. During the course of the service he moved up and down the aisles, squatting on his camp stool and looking most solemn and engrossed. Everyone was impressed. Later, with a twinkle in his eye, he confessed to the organist that he didn't know if he learned anything but he thought he had sold the committee.

Holtkamp did have a delightful sense of humor, albeit a bit sharp at times, in keeping with his outspoken nature. Frequently he would tease organists, especially about their desire for instruments larger than he considered necessary. Perhaps he was reminded of such organists when he learned of a novel aspect of the new Flentrop in the Bush-Reisinger Museum at Harvard University. The organ includes three alternate sets of pipes stored in special boxes by the organ so that an organist may remove a stop and replace it with something different. Holtkamp's reaction to these "convertible" stops, as reported by E. Power Biggs was, "Better keep this quiet or every organist will want a batch of convertibles."[18]

Holtkamp also enjoyed and cultivated contacts with other organ builders. This interest in knowing and learning from his colleagues, as well as the immediate threat to organ building in America posed by the advent of World War II, led him to encourage a gathering of interested persons in Ann Arbor, Michigan, in December 1941, which resulted in the founding of the Associated Pipe Organ Builders of America. Finn Videro reports how Holtkamp once confessed to him that one reason he enjoyed the APOBA gatherings was that he could pose a question to people whom he suspected of having differing ideas, just to get an argument going. Then he would sit quietly in the corner of the sofa to enjoy the altercation and see what he could learn from the clash of ideas.[19]

With the end of the war, and the surge in contracts postponed because of the war, Holtkamp's life revolved even more around his business and his friends, the organists, organ builders and others who appreciated and stimulated his art. In November 1948 he divorced his wife Margaret, ending a marriage of 20 years, and shortly thereafter took up residence in a small apartment above his shop. The children were grown and on their own, and as his interests centered more and more upon organ building and the shop, this arrangement seemed a natural one to him. Often he would encourage the staff to work odd hours so that there would be some activity in the shop on evenings and weekends. Visitors were often amazed at the informality with which the factory was organized, especially when comparing it to other larger organ firms or other industries with which they were familiar.[20]

As the firm prospered in the years after the war, it was

now possible to plan for a visit to Europe, which provided the first opportunity for Holtkamp to see and hear the instruments he had studied through his library of books and extensive record collection. Arranged primarily by Fenner Douglass, this first European trip in 1951 included visits to Holland, northern Germany, Switzerland, and Alsace, ending with a short time in England.[21] The first trip was followed by others in 1953, 1954, 1957, and 1960. During these later trips he often arranged to visit or travel with European friends, especially the organists Finn Videro and André Marchal, whom he knew and respected greatly. While he was interested in what he saw and heard, his own work seemed little influenced or changed by these visits. His time of experimentation was over and the encounters with the instruments, performers, and builders of Europe were as an equal, interested in learning but sure of his own abilities. D. A. Flentrop has an interesting perspective on Holtkamp at this point in his career.

> I do not have the feeling that I have influenced Walter Holtkamp in any way. He had made himself before I learned to know him. He didn't like to be influenced at all, this may be the main reason he didn't change much and didn't want to make encased organs. Why should he? He made excellent instruments in his way and he didn't want to experiment in other ways with the risk of losing part of the excellence he had gained in his own specific way.[22]

In the fall of 1956, Walter Holtkamp, Jr., joined the firm and prepared to continue the work of his father and grandfather. Walter Holtkamp, Sr., continued to guide the production of organs in his stable, mature, and articulated style into the early 1960s. On the evening of 10 February 1962, while completing negotiations for a new organ for Lakewood Presbyterian Church, Holtkamp was taken ill and died early the next day. Like his father before him, he died while engaged in the work that was so great a part of his life.

On 17 February 1962 a memorial service was held at St. Paul's Episcopal Church, Cleveland Heights, with organists Arthur Poister, Walter Blodgett, and Fenner Douglass paying musical tribute to him on one of his favorite instruments. Friends came from many parts of the country to honor the man whose work, ideas, and ideals had so strongly influenced them and the course of organ building in America.

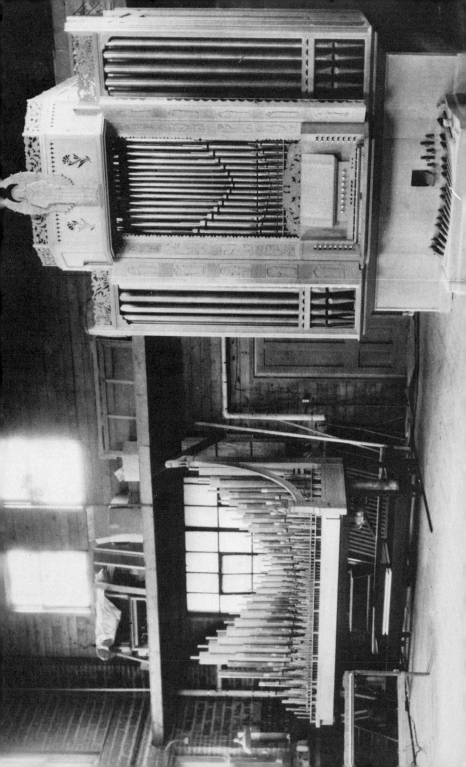

2
Years of Transition
(1931-1933)

The death of Henry Holtkamp in 1931 ended an era for the firm of Votteler-Holtkamp-Sparling, and came at the end of an era in American organ building as well. A glance at the stoplist of the 1931 installation in the Detroit Society of the New Church (see appendix A) shows how an age of electricity, providing such ease in unification and duplexing, and an emphasis on unison tone, had influenced the Holtkamps. Of the 21 ranks in the stoplist, 15 were 8' registers, 3 were 16' registers, 2 were 4' registers and 1 was a 2' register. This organ, designed as the 1930s were dawning, is typical of the work of the Holtkamps, father and son, at that time.

A hint of the changes to come can be found through a comparison of the organs for All Saints Church, Minot, North Dakota, and Brunnerdale Seminary, Canton, Ohio. The organ in Minot was one of the last instruments to be designed and installed under the direction of Henry Holtkamp. The stoplist reveals an instrument of nine ranks, highly unified and with little concern for any kind of chorus or ensemble. The organ was installed in a chamber with all pipes in a single swell box, except the Great Diapason and Dulciana and the Pedal Subbass. The organ at Brunnerdale Seminary was one of the first instruments to be designed, sold, voiced, and installed completely under the direction of Walter Holtkamp. The contract was signed on 1 January 1932. While of similar size, eight ranks, and still highly unified, the Brunnerdale organ is quite different. It provides a reed voice, replaces one muddy stopped wood bass with a 16′ Salicional, and provides an 8′ voice in the Pedal other than stopped flute. The wind pressures are lowered, and both manual divisions have a 2′ voice other than a flute.

The most significant difference between these two instruments is not to be found by comparing stoplists. The Great at Brunnerdale has what Holtkamp called a "Diapason Chorus," and this chorus is unenclosed and unencased.[1] Across the back wall of the chapel the pipes of the Great Diapason and Octave are placed upon an A-chest, the pipes of each rank in a double row, treble in front of bass to heighten the effect of progression from tallest pipe in the center to the shorter pipes at the sides of the chest. The Pedal Subbass is placed at either end of the Great chest with the tallest four pipes facing forward and the rest facing towards the sides of the gallery. The bottom octaves of the Diapason are decorated with a fleur-de-lis painted at the top of each pipe, and the front of the chest is covered with a carved panel bearing the words, "Et Non Impedias Musicam," the first use of what was to become a Holtkamp trademark. This little two-stop division with its pedal bass is probably the first unenclosed, unencased division to be installed in America in modern times.[2]

In a letter to The Very Reverend Ignatius Wagner of Brunnerdale Seminary dated 5 March 1932, Holtkamp writes, "You will be interested to know that the *Diapason Chorus* [italics mine] of the organ for Brunnerdale proved to be of unusual interest to local musicians this past week. We had that section of the organ hooked up to a small keyboard and it was tried by many organists both Protestant and Catholic." In a letter he writes of his concept of flute tone in relation to the rest of the instrument. "Our ideas of Flute tone were led astray by the late Robert Hope Jones. Too much and too heavy a Flute tone gives the organ that wooly character which interferes so much with the Diapason flavor we are after."[3]

Although disappointing by today's standards, the Brunnerdale organ is quite remarkable for its time. Both string registers are reasonably warm, not thin and scratchy; the Gamba is almost a small principal. The flute is clean and not at all thick. This organ demonstrates that Holtkamp was thinking about bringing his instruments out of chambers and into the room in which they were to sound, providing for a more gentle, unforced sound through lower pressures, and reducing the weight and thickness of the ensemble both by the voicing and scaling of the pipes, and by the choice of registers. While Brunnerdale gives us clues to Holtkamp's thinking at the time he assumed control of the firm, the challenge today is to reconstruct the thought processes that led Walter Holtkamp to move in the directions hinted in the Brunnerdale organ. This challenge is especially difficult for us who assume so much about the basics of good organ design and construction, principles understood by so few in the 1920s and '30s, especially in America.

For some time the Holtkamps, Henry and Walter, had been aware of the organ reform movement in Germany. They both read German well and had studied Albert Schweitzer's pamphlet, *The Art of Organ Building and Organ Playing in Germany and France*, "the first and basic document of the German organ reform movement."[4] In 1928 they discovered an article on the "Praetorius" organ at Freiburg, built by Walcker in 1921 according to the specifications given by Praetorius in *Syntagma Musicum*, Vol. 2, *De Organographia* (1619). The article precipitated a correspondence with Rudolph Barkow in Charlottenburg, a suburb of Berlin. This correspondence between Henry Holtkamp, the 70-year-old American organ builder, and Barkow, the young student of mechanical engineering and organ enthusiast, is most interesting, and continued for about two years. During this time much information about contemporary German and American ideas on organ building passed back and forth. Henry Holtkamp wanted to know what the Germans meant when they used terms like *Rückpositiv, Brustpositiv,* and *Oberpositiv.* Barkow rsponded with information, pictures, and diagrams including some of reasonably important historic German organs. These questions and a request for a description, "excluding appearances" of the "Renaissance-Orgel" and "Barock-Orgel," also were asked of Dr. Carl Elis, whose article about the Praetorius organ appeared in one of the German journals on organ and church music that came to the Holtkamp shop. The answers provided by these men, while so mundane to us today, must have been remarkable to the Holtkamps reading them in the late 1920s. In return for this information, Henry Holtkamp provided answers to questions raised by the Germans about American organs. They were interested in knowing about our Diaphone, Ludwigtone, and Erzähler. Dr. Elis also asks, with a comment questioning potential effectiveness, about the 64' Gravissima using the German phrase, "Was ist das?" A good question indeed!

While still listing organs with Diaphones and even Gravissimas, the American organ journals of the time were beginning to mention the Schulze, Cavaillé-Coll, and Willis schools of organ building "based on the idea of cohesive ensemble, with clarity and balance on and between all manuals and pedals."[5] The expression "Diapason Chorus" began to appear rather frequently, and interest in the

English Cathedral organs seemed to mount. Walter Holtkamp was interested in the English style of organ building and in the idea of a Diapason Chorus. Yet he found that many ideas expressed in the American journals of the time appeared to be in conflict with much that Schweitzer and other German sources seemed to be saying. In Schweitzer he recognized "a man of not only complete competence in the field which won his respect, but also a man whose approach to the problem was totally non-English. This aroused his curiosity."[6]

By the late 1920s, his father's increasing age placed even greater responsibility upon Walter Holtkamp, and he became convinced that organ building would soon cease to be a partnership with his father and become a life work of his own. To better prepare himself, he began assembling a library on organ building and organ music. He arranged for translations of certain French treatises on the subject to complement the German volumes he could read for himself. He began to study the laws and behavior of sound waves along with other acoustical matters, and Dayton C. Miller's *Science of Musical Sound* was a constant companion. Sittler speculates that the interest in getting the pipes out in the open came in part from this study of the behavior of sound waves.[7]

An indirect influence on Holtkamp's thinking was the stock-market crash of 1929. Since contracts for organs and negotiations for new instruments involve some lead time, the darkest days for the firm did not come until the early 1930s. The psychological impact of the crash, especially heightened for Holtkamp because he observed the loss of his wife's inheritance, reinforced his tendency to question America's constant enthralment with anything bigger and more complex. Perhaps there was virtue in something simple and honest. In his notes for a book on organ building, the unfinished manuscript of which is in the company archives, there is a clipping from an issue of the *Saturday Evening Post,* which quotes a famous and successful oilman lauding the virtues of simplicity as "the master key to success—no matter whether it be success in the temporal or spiritual sphere."[8]

The interest in a simpler style of organ building influenced the design of the organ for St. John's Evangelical Lutheran Church, Cleveland, contracted for on 14 March 1932. While continuing the practice of fleshing out the Great through borrows from other divisions as shown in earlier Holtkamp specifications, such complexity is much reduced. This instrument provided independent registers at sufficient pitches in each manual division to produce an ensemble without unification. The Great even boasts a mixture. Webber rightly observes that one must examine this stoplist in the light of the typical two-manual organ of the day, and cites another nearby Lutheran church, which installed a two-manual, 17-stop Aeolian in 1931. "Of the manual stops all were of 8' pitch with the exception of one timid little flute."[9]

Yet Brunnerdale and St. John's along with their peers provide but the smallest hints of the remarkable instruments that were to come from the Holtkamp shop in the years 1933 and 1934. These years saw the organ for Cleveland's Our Lady of Peace Roman Catholic Church, the Rückpositiv for the Cleveland Museum of Art, and then in quick succession the organs for St. John's Roman Catholic Church, Covington, Kentucky, and St. Mary's Roman Catholic Church and Miles Park Presbyterian Church of Cleveland. With these five instruments, Walter Holtkamp signaled a complete break with the recent past and embarked on a new direction in organ building for his firm, a direction radical and without parallel in its time.

3
Radical Years
(1933-1945)

With few contracts in hand, and in order to give expression to his evolving ideas, Walter Holtkamp decided to build a sample instrument that was completed in time to be shown at the American Guild of Organists convention in Cleveland in 1933. For financial reasons, and because his erecting room was small, it was essential to keep the instrument rather small. This decision was easy to accept, since it complemented Holtkamp's personal tendencies to prefer the small to the large and the simple to the complex. The final design evolved into a one-manual, electro-pneumatic organ with a manual compass from GG to g^3, 61 keys, divided at b. The manual registers were enclosed in a box with shutters on the front, top, and sides of the case, with the Pedal Cello providing visible, speaking pipes in the case. A Cleveland architect and designer, Richard Rychtarik, was engaged to prepare a gothic case design. The organ was modified into a more conventional two-manual instrument for installation in Cleveland's Our Lady of Peace Roman Catholic Church, where one can still see this most beautiful instrument and wonder if it might not be one of the handsomest organs made anywhere in the year 1933.

While the tonal modifications make it impossible to judge the tonal effectiveness of the original experiment,

Holtkamp must have learned much from this adventure. The learning process was aided by the interest and support of two Cleveland musicians, Arthur Quimby and Melville Smith.

> As an energizing stimulus during the months that this organ was under construction the counsel, musicianship, strict taste, and almost phenomenal patience of Melville Smith when the instrument was finally in playing condition was of the first importance. For literally hours, weeks, and months on end an analysis of the organ was carried on by submitting it to the trial of producing clear and meaningful sounds. Smith played and H listened. The one-manual instead of an embarrassment proved to be to a musician of Smith's calibre an actual challenge. This creative companionship of Smith and H reminds one of a sentence from Schweitzer's Bach, "It seems as though the music of Bach is destined to reform not only the organists but the organ builders and win them away from the loud tone organ to the instrument of rich and beautiful tone." Smith played music of all periods, and even upon an organ of what would generally be termed ridiculous size, it all seemed to "go." At long last H himself perceived a beauty of this music which he had never been fully conscious of before. He actually *heard* the music for the first time—heard the clear, distinct second entry of the fugue for instance as something besides mere increased tonal complexity; found himself actually awaiting the fugal line to speak out again; in Keats' words, "bold and clear."[1]

Arthur Quimby had come to Cleveland in 1925 to be Curator of Musical Arts at the Cleveland Museum of Art. In 1930 he was instrumental in arranging for his friend and classmate (Harvard 1920), Melville Smith, to join him in Cleveland, first as Lecturer, then as Associate Professor of Music, at Flora Stone Mather College of Western Reserve University. Smith had extensive European study with Nadia Boulanger in Paris and was especially interested in early keyboard music. Quimby intoduced him to Walter Holtkamp at the Cleveland Museum in 1931. Smith was playing a series of five recitals, exploring organ music of the

sixteenth and seventeenth centuries at the invitation of Quimby, and Mrs. Melville Smith believes this series to be the occasion for the first meetings of the three.[2]

The musical activities at the Museum in the early 1930s offered much to an organ builder interested in hearing the literature for his instrument, especially literature other than the usual recital fare of the day. In 1930 André Marchal was invited to present a series of all-Bach recitals, and in 1931 the aforementioned Smith series took place. In the winter of 1933–34 a series of recitals presenting the entire organ works of J. S. Bach was presented by Quimby in partnership with Smith.

The friendship of Holtkamp with Quimby and Smith ("The Troika" was the name given them by Joseph Sittler, who enjoyed being "the mediator between the two empires" of organ builder and organ player while in Cleveland in the 1930s) marked the beginning of many friendships with organists. Sittler writes of these friendships and quotes Holtkamp about the importance of hearing his friends play the instruments upon which he was experimenting.

In all of the foregoing it must be said that for H the "proof of the pudding" was the actual hearing of the music. Very little of the theoretical and very much of the practical entered into development. There began during these years that friendly alliance with practicing musicians including orchestra and choral men as well as organists which has persisted to this time. He perceived them to be his natural professional friends. They wanted to play music of the classical period of organ composition but found that this music could not possibly be communicated meaningfully upon the contemporary organs available to their use. Out of this acquaintanceship H formed the conviction that his innovations in organ design, which had heretofore been deferential, were changes in line with the inevitable direction in the whole field of music. ("My contact with non organists and with musicians who were organists only incidentally made it clear to me that simon-pure oganists were inhibited and somehow felt that organ music and organ playing was governed by a separate or special set of musical and acoustical laws and existed apart from general life. Also I learned that 20th Century organists were not held in high esteem by musicians in general. And that the instrument, the organ (20th Century) was not recognized by general musicians as a serious instrument. Further, many outstanding 20th Century composers were *not* composing for the organ and of course we know that this is a complete reversal as the composers of old were very fond of the organ. This all worried me and led me to look at the organ dispassionately. It also caused me to seek professional and artistic companionship with all instrumentalists and to study the traditions of all instruments but especially of course, the keyboard instruments. John Challis, the harpsichord maker and player, is a case in point. John has indirectly contributed much to the Holtkamp organ."[3]

The friendship of the organists Quimby and Smith with Holtkamp prompted them to turn to him with a request to provide an instrument to be added to the Museum's 1922 Skinner for use in their projected series of Bach recitals during the 1933–34 season. The lessons learned from the experimental instrument later installed in Our Lady of Peace Roman Catholic Church provided the basis for what evolved as the first Rückpositiv to be built in America in modern times. The new division was received well, as the reviews of its inaugural on 25 October 1933 made clear. This installation was the first to attract wide attention to Holtkamp. An article appeared in *The Diapason*, in which Carleton Bullis wrote, "One was able to listen attentively to a whole program of Bach music without feeling bored, so delightfully sparkling and incisive and alive was the effect of the music."[4] A longer article in *The American Organist* of December 1933 provided a complete description of the new division and its location on the gallery rail of the Museum's Garden Court, in front of the main organ in the gallery and behind the player's back. Pipework of the division, provided on loan by the builder, stood on an electro-pneumatic ventil chest. The 4' Prestant was made of copper, probably

St. John's Church, Covington, Kentucky, erected in the factory

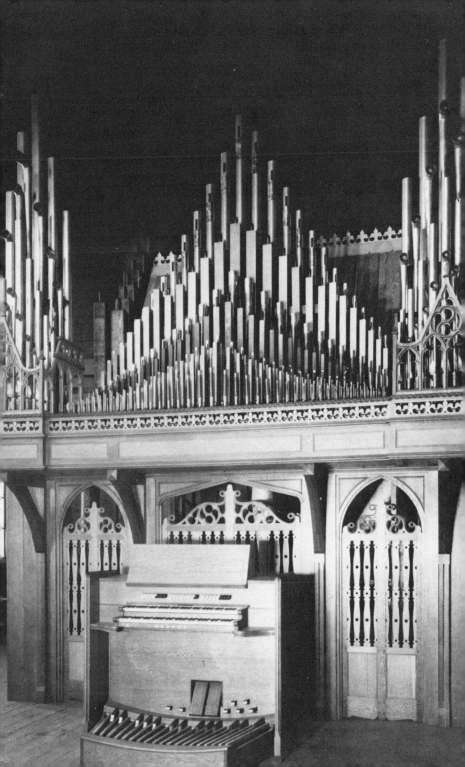

the first such in America. The photograph (Plate 1) showing the Museum Rückpositiv and the experimental organ standing side by side in the Holtkamp shop dramatically documents what remarkable things were occurring in the small organ factory on Cleveland's near West Side.

With the success of the Rückpositiv at the Museum to strengthen his conviction that he was on the right track, three other instruments followed in quick succession in 1934. Like the Museum Rückpositiv, all were totally unencased, even to the placement of the swell box completely in the open with its moving shutters for all to see (and many to react violently against). The best known of the three is the instrument for St. John's Roman Catholic Church, Covington, Kentucky, designed in collaboration with consultant Parvin Titus. Installed in the rear gallery of a large, high basilica, the instrument remains to this day a revelation.

> Architecturally, this little instrument was just as daring as the work then being done by Le Corbusier, Mendelsohn, Mes van der Rohe, A. and G. Perret and others, and it is just as functional. It states in simple terms that it is a small organ of two manual divisions—one enclosed, the other open—and a Pedal division; the open division stands front and center, flanked by the towers of pedal pipes. It is a striking example of the beneficial results of serious and conscientious study of lines, massing, silhouette and detail—results which are brought into sharper focus when compared with the sad and depressing American organ installations of the period.[5]

In design this organ represents the final break with earlier Holtkamp building. "Simplicity marks the instrument in all details, both structural and tonal."[6] The instrument is completely straight except for one 16′ manual register borrowed to pedal, thus beginning a tradition of almost complete avoidance of unification or duplexing, a consistent policy not adopted by any other American builder until quite recently, even though all affirm the great importance of such a policy from a tonal standpoint. The Great and Swell stand on divided chests, making possible different wind pressures for bass and treble portions of each rank, and providing for the remarkable array of pipes in the central section of the organ drawn from only the five ranks of the Great. Tonally, the instrument, while gentle in this large building, is amazing. Walter Blodgett expressed my reactions in a more poetic way than I when he described for me his visit to the organ.

> When I went to Covington recently I was struck—in Florence there is a Michaelangelo Museum there which includes several great hunks of stone which he had started to carve and then stopped and all I could think of when I played that organ was here is one of those; sort of started but the figure had not yet emerged. Everything was there in principle, not developed but in embryo. It was a little disappointing because it seemed timid at the console. Then Gerre Hancock played it and I was amazed at how enormous it sounded downstairs—as early as that; the sensitivity that he had to an acoustic stituation and to build for it.[7]

The St. Margaret's organ followed St. John's and, while much smaller, was the same in design philosophy, complete to the 4' copper Prestant in the Great. The organ for Miles Park was the last of the organs in the momentous year 1934 and is the largest of the three. While not as publicized as St. John's, and placed in a much smaller and drier room, the instrument is to this day a beautiful experience in sight and sound. It is placed right in the center of the front of the church, above and behind the choir where its exposed pipes and swell mechanism are visible for all to see. After using it regularly for four years as organist of the church while an undergraduate student, my admiration for the flexibility and musicality of this instrument remains unbounded. It is a big, bright-sounding instrument that meets the needs of the church well and provides more than ample resources for the leading of hymns, accompaniment of anthems, and a substantial portion of the organ literature as well. The Pedal division is remarkably complete for a two-manual organ of its size, especially one of the early 1930s, and even includes the unusual Great to Pedal 5⅓' coupler, which is found on other of the early Holtkamps. The color provided by the mutations and reeds is a revelation for an instrument of its size and epoch; the inclusion of the Cromorne in the Swell was a first for Holtkamp and probably for America as well. It was scaled after an example in the Emile Rupp book and sounded like a classic French Cromorne. [8]

Mention was made in the preceding paragraph of the unusual coupler on the Miles Park organ. As early as 1934 Holtkamp considered each division as a complete ensemble, for which too many couplers would only upset the tonal balance. For this reason he did not provide couplers 16-8-4 for everything to everywhere, the norm on most organs in 1934 and still the norm (unless specifically instructed otherwise) for some builders today who should know better. The couplers provided on the Miles Park instrument are typical of those on most of Holtkamp's organs of this period (GP 8, 5⅓, 4; SP 8; S 16; SG 16, 8; and G 4). When the Great had no stop above 4' pitch, a coupler was provided to give the potential for a brighter ensemble. The Swell to Great 16' was included, perhaps to provide for a 16' reed sound in the ensemble, but the Swell to Great 4' was removed to assure that the Mixture in the Swell could not be made to scream. The Great to Pedal 4' was usually present if the Great 4' was provided. The unusual 5⅓' coupler appeared on some of the two-manual instruments of the time and did provide for a rich pedal sound.

With the five organs of 1933–34 Holtkamp was estab-

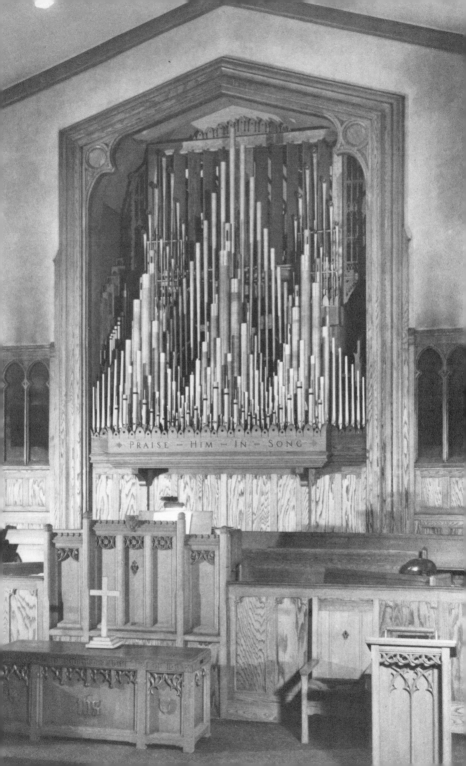

PRAISE — HIM — IN — SONG

lished upon his course in organ building. In writing of the Covington organ for the *American Organist* at the request of its editor, T. Scott Buhrman, Holtkamp articulated what he was doing at this point in his development.

> [The] principles demonstrated in the building of the organ for St. John's Church in Covington are the practical application of a credo. The efforts of my firm during the past four years, of which the building of the Rückpositiv for The Cleveland Museum of Art has probably been the most publicized, have been directed toward bringing the organ out into the open where it can reveal its true character. A new technique has had to be developed and this has often led us to the camps of the Silbermanns and Cavaillé-Colls. We have borrowed freely from these old masters but always with an ear for modern conditions. Stripping the instrument of inhibition and sophistication fulfills modern tenets and at the same time restores many of the most desirable primitive features.[9]

Writing of Covington, Sittler observes, "Here is a perfect adaptation of 'form to function.' A firm believer in smaller organs placed in more advantageous positions, and an unremitting enemy of the general practice of stuffing organs into holes in the wall, Holtkamp here built an organ incorporating all of his own growing conceptions."[10] These words could be applied to St. Margaret's and Miles Park as well and provide a perfect verbal capstone to the end of the most radical phase of Holtkamp's development as an organ builder.

In 1935, building with inexorable logic upon the lessons learned the past few years and his continuing study of European ideas in organ building, Holtkamp made his final radical move as an organ builder and returned to mechanical action. He implemented a project to construct a small one-manual organ which he called the Portative. This instrument, with tracker action on a slider chest, inaugurated America's second tracker period. This second era of Ameri-

can organ building utilizing mechanical action did not really become established, however, until the middle to late 1960s, so the Portative, an instrument 30 years ahead of its time, remained a lonely orphan in what was still an electro-pneumatic age.[11]

The key compass of the Portative was G to g^3, with a tonal design providing for three registers; 8' Quintadena (metal), 4' Prestant, and III Cornet. The registers were activated by a series of pedal levers, much like those controlling registers on a harpsichord, and the Cornet was provided with an individual slider for each rank to allow for greater flexibility. The pipes of the Cornet were covered by a small box with movable slats on top so that a degree of dynamic control was possible.

The visual design of the instrument was just as daring in its own way as the mechanical design. The base of the instrument incorporated a small blower, so the Portative was a complete unit in itself. With remarkably simple, clean and uncluttered lines, the Portative looked like it belonged in a space designed by one of the pioneering architects of the time. For this instrument Holtkamp again engaged Richard Rychtarik to do the visual design. At this point in his career Holtkamp was not yet sure of his architectural instincts and often called upon architects and designers whom he respected to work with him. After World War II, he no longer felt this need for assistance and normally did his own visual designs. Factory records are unclear as to the exact number of Portative organs produced, but evidence suggests that as many as seven were constructed during 1935–36. Their present locations are not all known, although one is at the Holtkamp shop and another at the Cleveland Museum of Art.[12]

The Portative was designed to sell for little more than a small unit organ or the new electric and electronic instruments just beginning to appear. Holtkamp proposed an honest, simple organ as an alternative to the complex, dishonest unit organs and the new pseudo-organs. The public was not interested. Sittler quotes Holtkamp on the Portative.

> This urge to natural, functional expression and the almost complete lopping off of encrustations has marked our work more and more. The Portative is a typical example of this direct design—even in spite of "no market." The prevailing market was for the unit organ with two manuals and pedal *but* with fewer pipes than the Portative.[13]

The years 1935 and 1936 must have been the most discouraging of all for Walter Holtkamp. There seemed to be "no market" for any of his ideas and the initial publicity surrounding the remarkable instruments of 1933–34 did not result in contracts that would allow him to continue his experimentation and growth. During this period the continuing interest, encouragement, and support of organists and friends Quimby and Smith must have been invaluable. The circle of friends grew to include Walter Blodgett, Russell Gee (faculty member of Western Reserve University) and Robert Noehren as well. Through Blodgett, who was to succeed Quimby at the Museum in 1942, came the next opportunity to build a Positiv division.

Walter Blodgett came to Cleveland in the early 1930s after graduating from Oberlin College, hoping to find a position in one of the many Cleveland churches that employed full-time musicians. He quickly established a reputation as a fine performer and as an articulate and erudite champion of the musical arts. In the middle 1930s, he was organist-choirmaster at St. James' Episcopal Church and asked Holtkamp to provide a Positiv division much like the Museum's to add to the existing organ. The small division of three registers on 2½ inches of wind pressure included another 4' copper Prestant. The division was placed on a side wall of the church above and behind the head of the organist. Later in the same year (1936) a contract was signed for a major revision of the 1927 Votteler organ in St. Philomena's Roman Catholic Church in Cleveland. Here Holtkamp's first Rückpositiv in a church was placed on the balcony railing with the rest of the organ located on either side of a large window in the gallery. While most of the pipes and action were reworked from the old organ, the Positiv was new except for a few extensively reworked ranks and certainly was the most interesting from a visual standpoint. Another interesting visual feature was the placing of the Pedal 4' Choralbass and Mixture on small chests on either side of the Positiv. The organ, dedicated on 5 May 1937, has not been maintained in recent years and is almost unplayable; this is exceptional, since most of the instruments from the 1930s, especially in Cleveland, are still well maintained and mostly in their original condition, a tribute to the durability both tonally and mechanically of these early Holtkamp instruments.

In 1937 Holtkamp was asked to provide a completely new organ for St. James' Church incorporating the Positiv he had already built. Blodgett's comments on the evolution of the stoplist are interesting. "I remember at St. James', money was not a concern. Yet we decided to build as small as possible yet having the proper character for each division."[14] The stoplist reveals a very small instrument with certain unusual features; for example, a Great 5⅓' Quint but no 4' register. At a later date the Swell was enlarged to include 2⅔' and 1³/s' mutations in addition to the original Kornet Mixture. The Positiv Cymbel had a 1³/s' pitch in it from the middle c up so the organ was amply provided with cornet registers, although the 1³/s' pitch in the Positiv Cymbel was eventually silenced.

The predilection for third-sounding partials and low quint mutations was a common characteristic of most Holtkamp organs of the thirties. As mentioned earlier, some included a Great to Pedal 5⅓' coupler. A study of the composition of the mixtures on the organs of this period reveals many third-sounding ranks and the introduction of 5⅓' and 10⅔' pitches at points early in the upward progression if measured by today's standards. No one has been able to provide a complete explanation for this predilection, although Blodgett speculates that Holtkamp was searching for a grave and big sound without the muddiness associated with many manual 16' registers of the time, and the thickness of many contemporary 8' flue registers. Blodgett's enjoyment of the color of third-sounding ranks in ensemble, along with the interest in early French music shared by all three of the organists closest to Holtkamp, may provide another clue to this characteristic of the Holtkamp organs of the period.[15]

Another remarkable instrument came from the shop in 1937, the organ for Emmanuel Lutheran Church, Rochester, New York. Here in this tiny instrument on slider chests we see the essence of the Holtkamp style of the 1930s. The Great of two stops is built upon an 8' Principal to provide support for congregational singing. The gentle 4' Flute, of ample scale but with small mouths, can sound with the 4' coupler without any scream. The Swell with its Cornet mixture is a reedless, reedy Swell. Again we find the 5⅓' Great to Pedal augmenting a division with two independent registers. All in all, this instrument is amazing for its versatility and especially for its musicality.

In the late 1930s Holtkamp finally received contracts for a few larger instruments that enabled him to work out his ideas in organ building on a somewhat larger scale. But it was not until just before World War II, in the organs for

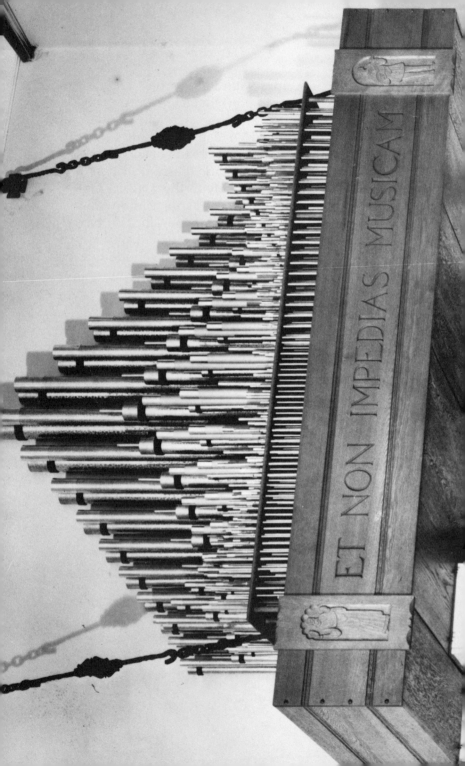

Baldwin Wallace College (Berea, Ohio), Fairmount Presbyterian Church (Cleveland), Olivet College (Olivet,
Michigan), and Our Lady of the Angels Roman Catholic
Church (Lakewood, Ohio), that we see his style, inaugurated with the five organs of 1933–34, now completely
articulated in these intruments at the end of this era of his
organ building.

The first, for Baldwin Wallace College, was contracted for
late in 1941, and was for three manuals and pedal, all except
large Pedal registers to be on slider chests. The second, for
Fairmount Presbyterian Church, was the first really large
organ Holtkamp built and is one of the few to include both
an enclosed Choir and Rückpositiv. The original console
was designed like those of the French Cavaillé-Coll instruments with stop knobs arranged in semicircular rows at
either side of the manuals. This unique console and other
details of the instrument reflect the interests and desires of
Russell Gee, then organist-choirmaster of the church.

The third organ was for Olivet College, and because of
this instrument Holtkamp came to know Joseph Bonnet,
one of the first European organists with whom he had a
personal acquaintance. Bonnet, famous French recitalist
and teacher, was touring America in 1942 and played the
opening recital at Olivet in February 1942. He was very
pleased with the instrument and wrote a letter of congratu-
lations to Walter Holtkamp that includes a sentence too
delightful to overlook. Writing in English, he observed, "I
am happy to see that your magnificent work is appreciated
more and more every day and that it pays to be courageous,
honest and sincere in spite of the many demagogues,
gangsters, mushrooms and other parasites and suckers of
musical art."[16]

Later in the same year a summer course in organ was
conducted by Bonnet at Olivet. There, with Holtkamp,

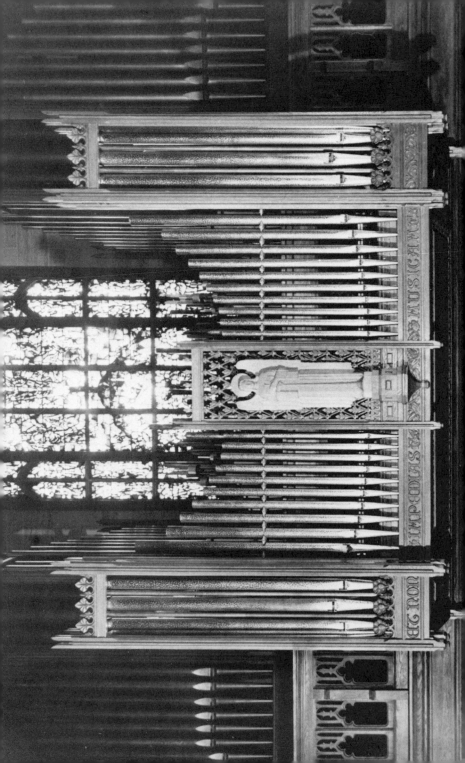

Bonnet speculated on the merits of good organ design and encouraged him to continue on his present course. An interesting stoplist of a "minimum" three-manual organ, later to be realized almost exactly at Cleveland's First Unitarian Church, was created by Bonnet, Blodgett and Holtkamp during this Olivet gathering.

The last and smallest of the four organs was for Our Lady of the Angels Church in Cleveland's western suburb of Lakewood. Although contracted for in 1941, it was not completed until 1942. Placed in the rear gallery of a handsome and resonant room, this instrument was one of Walter Holtkamp's favorites.

With the advent of World War II the construction of new organs ceased in this country, although a few more instruments previously contracted for and a few rebuilds left the shop during the war years. Of these, one deserves mention, that for the First Unitarian Church, Cleveland, where Walter Blodgett was organist-choirmaster. Built to a modification of the specification proposed at Olivet, it was most interesting for its new style of console—the first of the now famous Holtkamp stop key consoles. Holtkamp often expressed his dissatisfaction with the construction of the consoles being built by most American firms. He proposed a smaller, simpler console that would encourage the organist to be a keyboardist, not the controller of a big machine.

> The console of the early 1900's was a huge monumental affair that came to perfection in the years 1910–1930 in the console of tremendous intricacy and overpowering impressiveness. The very appearance of the console gave the player a machine-approach to his instrument. And this H conceived to be abhorrent. He therefore made a constant effort to reduce the console to minimum size; eliminate all possible gadgets; and wherever possible to make it contiguous with the instrument itself.[17]

At First Unitarian, the cramped space available for console

and choir provided him with the impetus to carry his convictions to their logical conclusion. As early as St. John's, Covington, and especially at St. James', Cleveland, the consoles reflect Holtkamp's interest in a more compact design. Now, with Blodgett's encouragement, Holtkamp built a console that was "keyboards and nothing else." With a shelf on each side for a hymnal and the stop tablets above, a compact and efficient console evolved. An interesting additional aspect of the Holtkamp console, the location of the intermanual coupler in a central section divorced from the manual stops, resulted from Blodgett's familiarity with the draw knob console arrangement placing such couplers above the keys. "I asked to have a central location and not have the couplers mixed up with the stops in the old Austin way."[18] A mechanical fringe benefit of this console design was the moving of all switching components out of the console due to limitations of space. Thus concern for compactness in relays, etc., was no longer a problem, and the large pneumatically activated switches could be placed where they would be easy to maintain and would not be disturbed if a console was made movable.

With the advent of World War II, an era in organ building ended for Holtkamp. The results of his experimentation, from consoles to wind chests, copper prestants to pedal posaunes, were all close by in Cleveland area churches, and he had time to reflect on his philosoplhy of organ building and speculate on his directions for the future. It was during this period that he worked most extensively on the previously mentioned manuscript for his book on organ building. Today the best insight into Holtkamp's thinking, as he began this short period of introspection precipitated by the war-time regulations forbidding the construction of new organs, is found in a lecture, *Present-Day Trends in Organ Building*, given at the Cleveland convention of the Music

Teachers National Association on 30 December 1940. Arranged by Arthur Poister, a new friend on the Oberlin Faculty, the talk was later printed as a part of the *Proceedings* of the MTNA for 1940 and provides the most complete statement by Holtkamp of his credo of organ building ever to appear in print.

After describing the American organ of the early twentieth century and observing that its worth seemed to be measured more by its size and mechanical ingenuity than by its tonal beauty, Holtkamp proposes his reasons for the failure of this style of organ building. "That the American organ of the last generation failed to endure, I attribute very much to the fact that it was too complete a break with the past, and that not enough composition of an enduring nature appeared for it to keep it alive as a new instrument."[19]

He then asserts that the best proving ground for the worth of an organ is the organ literature, and that the single most important, though not the only, test of an organ's worth is its ability to recreate the music of Bach. Other composers' music must sound good too. "Thus we see that the ultimate objective is to build an organ today which will reproduce the worthwhile organ music of all ages."[20]

Holtkamp gives five principles upon which the organ building of the future should be based. These ideas reflect the basic trend back towards the earlier conception of the organ as a smaller, simpler and more "intimate keyboard instrument for meticulous hands and feet."[21]

1. The organ must be located properly, directly in the room with the listeners.

Can you imagine even for an instant the master contrapuntists of old composing their great pieces for organs which growl and roar from the cavernous organ chambers, attics and basements in which the twentieth century organ builder is often forced to incarcerate his pipes, and with the notes running together and smearing to such an extent that his carefully worked out composition becomes just so much confusion?[22]

2. The wind pressure must be lowered because "in general, low-pressure tones are good chorus tones and blend well with their fellow tones."[23]

3. Instruments must be reduced in size. "An organ of modest proportions, located in a natural position in relation to the auditiorium, as well as to the chorus or orchestra, is musically more effective than a large organ which due to its bulk must be buried away someplace within the masonry of the building."[24]

4. The texture of organ tone must be enriched through reducing the number of fundamental or unison-tone registers and increasing the number of registers of overtone pitch. "In fact, the central idea of the contemporary organ movement, as I see it, is the re-establishment of a series of related pipes or tones; in effect a more or less complete harmonic series for each key as the basis or unit of consideration."[25]

5. The organ must again be constructed with key-chamber chests. "The natural way to blow two or more pipes and make them sound as one is for the blower to take them in his mouth, so to speak, or at least to cause them to be blown by or from a common air chamber."[26]

This then was Holtkamp's credo at the end of his first ten years of organ building. A glance backward over the instruments produced during this decade demonstrates how close Holtkamp had come to effecting his ideals as an organ builder. As early as Brunnerdale Seminary he began to bring his instruments out of closets and chambers into the room in which they were to be heard. He had lowered wind pressures and was building smaller, less complicated organs. The increase of upperwork, especially mutations and mixtures, and a corresponding decrease in unison tone was apparent in all his instruments from 1933 on. Experiments with electro-pneumatic slider chests and even tracker action had begun in attempts to reintroduce the keychamber wind chest to America. The time for a consolidation of experiments and the evolution of a mature style of organ building was at hand.

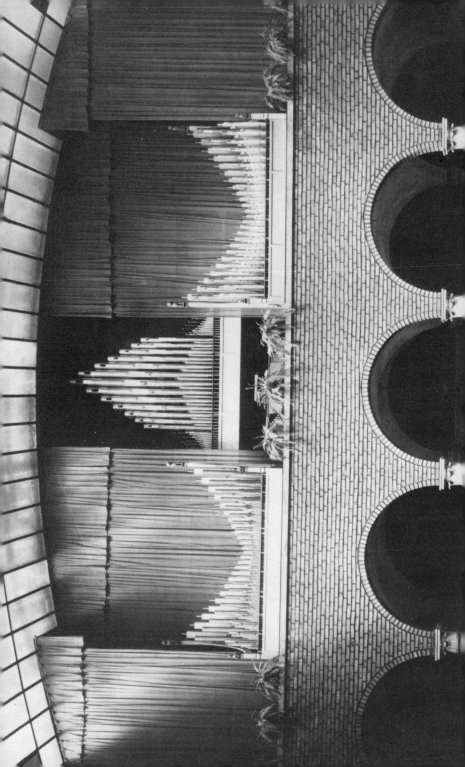

4
Towards A Mature Style
(1945-1950)

With the end of World War II in 1945, American organ builders could return to organ building, and pipes and wind chests quickly replaced war material as the builders rushed to meet the backlog of orders generated by the interruption of the war. Holtkamp's first important postwar contract was for the rebuilding of the organ at the Cleveland Museum of Art.

The Museum's 1922 Skinner was showing signs of age and as the mechanical troubles became more serious, Walter Blodgett was able to persuade the Museum trustees to raise funds for the repair and tonal revision of the organ. "Many liberal tycoons of business contributed on the basis that the machine did not work. This was fortunate because I got nowhere on the matter of tone."[1] The Rückpositiv, added to the Museum organ in 1933, had remained a part of the instrument and was on permanent loan from Holtkamp. Blodgett now hoped to effect a tonal revision to bring the rest of the instrument into greater tonal compatibility with the proven and successful Rückpositiv.

A generous gift from Mr. and Mrs. E. J. Kulas[2] together with other funds provided by the Museum trustees made possible the contracting of the work in 1945. The shape of the new tonal scheme was influenced by the funds available, and after the entire instrument was removed to the Holtkamp factory, experiments were conducted there to determine which sets of pipes could be reused, often after extensive reworking by the voicers. The original Rückpositiv was retained and finally paid for. The completed instrument was opened in November of 1946 and caused an immediate stir. It remained an organ of especial interest for years, and visitors came "sometimes by carloads, from as far away as Texas schools."[3]

Certainly the most famous visitor to the Museum was Albert Schweitzer, who visited Ameica for a speech at the University of Chicago in the summer of 1949. He had read of the original installation of the Rückpositiv at the Museum and had written Holtkamp in 1934 to congratulate him for his pioneering work.

> Bravo for the first Rückpositiv in America. I congratulate. That is work for Truth. And struggle for beautiful intonation against strong intonation. And for the Schleiflade!—may you find imitators! Truth will triumph one day. . . . And only one expressif clavier, not two ones! Well go on to fight for Truth. From heaven J. S. Bach and César Franck will look upon you with kindness![4]

Upon arrival in this country, Schweitzer specifically requested an opportunity to visit the Museum to see the organ, the only American instrument he asked to play.[5] While in Cleveland he visited Our Lady of the Angels Church as well. The next day the *Plain Dealer* reported his visit and quoted him, "All organists and organs will go to Hades for seven years. But Mr. Holtkamp will not go to Hades."[6]

The Museum, visited by the famous and the curious, and the scene of so many musical triumphs, was Holtkamp's most important laboratory. He never had the funds to do much experimentation other than through his contracts for instruments. With the continuing interest and encouragement of his circle of organist friends, and especially through

Walter Holtkamp with Albert Schweitzer at the Cleveland Museum of Art

the kind cooperation of Blodgett, he was able to experiment on the Museum instrument.

In the 1946 revision, the Positiv was placed at the left of the console and balanced by a slider chest at the right of the console with portions of the upperwork of the Pedal division. The Great (the largest portion on a new slider chest) was placed in the center above and behind the console with the expressive divisions and the balance of the Pedal on either side and behind the open Positiv and Pedal chests. While this visual arrangement remained essentially the same until the instrument was removed to be redesigned for installation in the Museum's new Gartner Auditorium in 1971, tonal revisions continued throughout the 1950s and '60s. The sudden death of Walter Holtkamp in 1962 interrupted plans for a major change to the Great Principal Chorus. Because the instrument's history was one of evolutionary change, Walter Holtkamp, Jr., agreed to complete the revisions as proposed. Later in 1966, more than a dozen of the original Skinner registers retained in earlier rebuilds were replaced with new pipes. Thus this organ, beginning with the first experiments with the Rückpositiv in 1933, played an important role in the development of Holtkamp's style as an organ builder.[7]

The late 1940s provided two additional opportunities for important contracts that were to prove central to the fortunes of the firm in the next decade, the organs for Warner Hall at Oberlin College and Crouse Hall at Syracuse University. These instruments, in design philosophy and even visual appearance, had their roots in the Museum organ. Such similarities are easily understood when one notes that they all were rebuilds and that the organists involved, Fenner Douglass, Grigg Fountain and Arthur Poister, were all familiar with and enthusiastic about the Museum instrument.

Arthur Poister had first met Walter Holtkamp when he joined the Oberlin faculty in the late thirties.

> Walter, when I got to Oberlin, called up and wanted to come out. We had lunch and talked—didn't talk too much organ, we just talked. He invited me to Cleveland; said he had an organ he was building putting his ideas into sound, a kind of demonstration. Invited me to bring students. So we went in and that was my introduction to Walter's ideas. It was like running into a brick wall; really revolutionary. As I look back at it now I wasn't that enthusiastic. I'd had my old organ, which was suave and romantic compared to this. But I didn't turn my nose and say nothing doing. I kept seeing Walter, listening and talking, and somehow it made sense.[8]

One of the students in Poister's class on the first visit to the shop was Fenner Douglass, who subsequently joined the Oberlin faculty when Poister accepted the invitation of Syracuse University to join its faculty in 1948. Grigg Fountain first met Holtkamp in the summer of 1945, at the urging of Poister, and cultivated his acquaintanceship upon joining the Oberlin faculty in the fall of 1946.[9]

The loss of Arthur Poister was a blow to the organ department of the Oberlin Conservatory, and one strategy proposed to counter this loss was the updating of the department's equipment. To this end a three-stage plan was implemented to rework the Skinner organ in Warner Concert Hall.[10] The first stage was a new Positiv and Pedal (completed in the winter of 1950); the second stage was a new Great on slider chest with some additional Pedal (completed 1951); the final stage was a revised Swell, Pedal reeds and reworking of some registers in the Choir (completed 1952).

Meanwhile at Syracuse, Poister and Holtkamp prepared plans for four organs; a new instrument for Crouse Hall incorporating certain pipes from the 1889 Roosevelt redone in 1928 by Estey, a radical rebuild of the Aeolian organ in

Hendricks Chapel, and two new practice instruments. The first instruments completed, Crouse Hall and one practice organ, were finished late in 1950.

The Cleveland Museum, Warner Hall, and Crouse Hall shared much in common. All were very large instruments for Holtkamp and incorporated some pipes and mechanism by earlier respected American builders. All were appreciated by their incumbent organists, if only because the builder doing the work was the first choice of the organists most directly involved. All, especially the latter two, were enormously influential because of the many students who heard and played upon them.

Physically, all were much alike as well. Warner and Crouse reveal the influence of the Museum design with the Positiv placed at the left of the console, Great directly above the console and Pedal upperwork from 8′ at the right of the console. With greater height at Warner and Crouse, a tower of pedal pipes could be placed behind the Great chest giving a slight asymmetrical touch to the balanced arrangement of Positiv to Great to Pedal from left to right. The Swell division in both instruments was placed high—at Crouse remarkably so—with Oberlin's Choir located under the Swell directly behind the Great.

The console at Warner and Crouse was made a part of the base of the case directly under the Great slider chest. At Oberlin the Skinner drawknob console was retained, the Positiv and Choir activated by the same knobs with a switch providing for either the Positiv or Choir, but not both. At Crouse a new drawknob console was made, one of the few ever constructed by Holtkamp. The aural sensation of the player at the console of Warner and Crouse was remarkably similar: the sound of the Great and Swell going out over one's head, the Positiv and Pedal clearly singing from the sides but still above the player.

Of these three remarkable instruments only Crouse remains. For me, hearing and playing this organ is an emotional experience, especially when my ears, while playing, are receiving sounds which stimulate memories of similar aural sensations from the Warner organ, now gone, which I knew and loved as a student. Therefore it is difficult for me to be an objective judge of the Crouse organ. Yet it can be said that Crouse is possessed of a big, bright, rich, vibrant, yet always clear sound enhanced by splendid acoustics. The instrument impresses one by its versatility, but especially by its musicality. A wide range of literature does sound effective on this instrument, even when judged by today's idealistic standards, which tend to frown upon an eclectic approach to organ building.

> Walter would come and he'd say, "I want to hear the organ." He'd say, "play a tune." I'd go and play and he'd say "play another." After awhile he'd sit there and not say anything, then he'd sit there and say, "sometimes it does and sometimes it doesn't." He was saying sometimes an organ sounds good, sometimes it doesn't but here it always does. He loved the acoustics of Crouse and the sound of the organ. But doesn't it say something when the organ builder likes to hear the organ.[11]

All three of these instruments, so musically and historically important to the story of Walter Holtkamp's art, are in many details not typical of his work. Perhaps this is because of the unique nature of the circumstances surrounding their design, all growing out of existing organs. In each case the organs had essentially new Great, Positiv and Pedal divisions with much of the Swell and the lower Pedal registers, except reeds, drawn primarily from the extant organs. In each case the resulting Swell seems larger than is typical for Holtkamp. All had an 8' Principal and big reeds in the Swell, a practice not continued on the mature instruments.

Each, especially those with a Choir, was more like the Harrison "American Classic" concept with larger Swell and more "romantic" voices than normal for Holtkamp. All were very large organs by Holtkamp standards.

An instrument more consistent with the evolutionary development of Holtkamp before World War II, but contemporary with the previously mentioned three, is located in St. Paul's Lutheran Church, Cleveland. Perhaps one reason for its clearer relationship to its prewar precursors is that it was essentially a new organ, although a few old ranks were incorporated in the pedal. Designed in 1947 with the assistance of consultants Walter Blodgett and Grigg Fountain, the St. Paul's Lutheran organ is one of the handsomest of the early postwar organs.

The sound is essentially big and assertive, with a Pedal division that seems overwhelming in the relatively small room. The Pedal division is also the largest division in the organ, as a glance at the console makes clear. Perhaps the most impressive division in sight and sound is the Rückpositiv. The Principals are of remarkably large scale with an unusually small scaled Rohrflöte for contrast. Grigg Fountain reports that D. A. Flentrop was especially struck by this Rückpositiv.

> I can testify that D. A. Flentrop was astounded on first hearing the Positiv section of the organ at St. Paul Lutheran Church that Holtkamp could produce that result without casework, without mechanical action, *and* never having heard any European organ—old or new.[12]

The design of this instrument follows logically from the instruments for Baldwin Wallace, Olivet and Our Lady of the Angels. The Swell still includes a Principal 8' and low pitched mixture along with the major manual reed. The Krummhorn on the Great does provide some reed color for this division but it is still not a major factor in the ensemble the way a Trumpet would be. The Krummhorn pipes are

Walter Holtkamp with Arthur Poister at the first "Martini" for Syracuse University

most interesting in that the half-length cylindrical resonators have a conical flared section at the top of the pipe
beginning at tenor C. Thus one might call the register a
Krummhorn-Trumpet. Here then is a hint of the next step
in Holtkamp's tonal evolution, the moving of the major
chorus reed to the Great.

Another instrument destined to be of far-reaching impact
was designed in these busy days of the late 1940s. This was
the small practice organ nicknamed the "Martini." As mentioned earlier, Arthur Poister left Oberlin College to join the
faculty of Syracuse University in the fall of 1948. The proposal for a reworked concert hall organ that was precipitated
by Positer's departure included a new practice-teaching
studio organ as well. As a kind of "audition" for the concert
hall contract, it was agreed first to purchase a Holtkamp
practice organ which, upon delivery, could provide a test-
ing of Holtkamp's work right in Oberlin.

To this end Holtkamp came to Oberlin in the early fall of
1948 to talk over the basic possibilities of a small organ for
practice purposes. Grigg Fountain relates that he,
Holtkamp, Arthur Poister, and Fenner Douglass had din-
ner at the old Oberlin Inn.

> We adjourned to a new apartment which Fenner and I had rented
> together—both being still single—and had Martinis and put down
> every possibility we could think of for cross duplication and unifica-
> tion to get the most for the least within what we then considered prime
> musical considerations. . . . The resulting organ was that first Martini
> model which reposed for many years at the head of the stairs on the
> second floor of Warner Hall. It was delivered in the early Spring of
> 1949 and was installed and finished by Lawrence Phelps who was then
> working for Holtkamp.[13]

The organ design, named the Martini in honor of the
cocktail that attended its conception, has proved to be remarkably durable. Over thirty of essentially the same design were in use in schools and a few churches across the

country at the time of Holtkamp's death in 1962. The essence of the design is a unit organ without the troubles normally associated with such an instrument. Since each rank of pipes is used only once on each manual division (with the exception of the Gedackt, which plays at 4' and 1⅓' on the upper manual) the problems of missing notes and out-of-balance registers so typical in unit instruments are avoided. The only major change in the original design was to extend the Quintaton down two octaves in the bass to become the 16' Pedal voice in place of the wood Gedackt, which was found to be somewhat big, heavy and slow of speech for the small spaces most typically occupied by these instruments. After the first four Martinis were made, this change became standard. (After the first two, an experiment with a composite rank of stopped wood to stopped metal with chimney at C25 to open metal at C49 was tried, but discarded again in favor of the original stopped wood to C49.)

With the installation of the organs at Oberlin and Syracuse, Holtkamp's fortunes took a new turn. These instruments, in prestigious institutions with respected organ departments, along with the new Museum organ, provided him with the recognition he had so long sought. Both Oberlin and Syracuse, because of their organists' faith in his abilities, had provided him with the opportunity to prove his worth in the testing-ground of an educational institution of national prominence. Both institutions, through their distinguished and talented graduates, assured a supply of enthusiastic, young organists ready to go out into America's churches and schools and champion his work. A decade of acclaim and prosperity was dawning. The time of trial and experimentation was over; the mature, confident organ builder was ready to provide instruments for the many converts to his style of organ building.

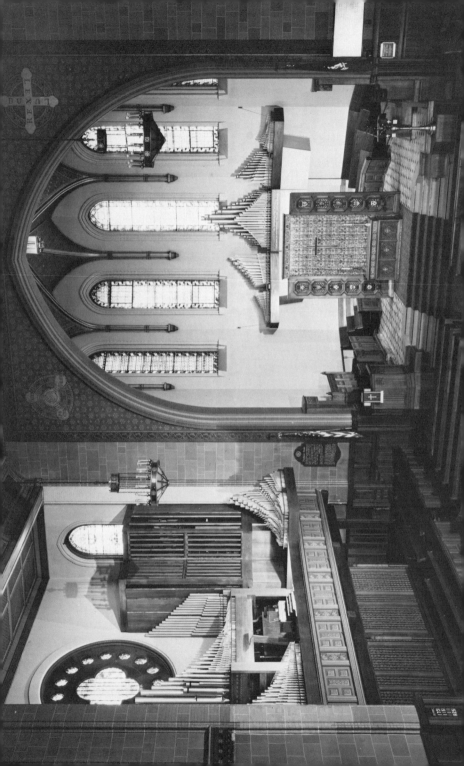

5
Mature Years
(1950-1962)

At the beginning of his last decade of organ building, Walter Holtkamp stood at the peak of his profession. John Fesperman has speculated, "Holtkamp's work was probably more influential than that of any other builder in the years just after World War II."[1] His reputation precipitated inquiries from across the country. His work was no longer primarily regional; he had become a national figure in organ building.

One inquiry of special importance for Holtkamp came regarding an organ for Battell Chapel at Yale University. Luther Noss, incumbent University Organist, had consulted with his friend G. Donald Harrison about the special musical and architectural problems in the chapel. The existing organ, a rebuilt and electrified Hook and Hastings, was located in a shallow side transept while the choir stalls and console were located in the apse. This arrangement presented problems of balance and synchronization for choir, organ, organist, and congregation. Noss and Harrison agreed that a double instrument seemed the best solution for the architectural problems and musical requirements. Harrison suggested that Holtkamp might be the person to build such an instrument. Holtkamp was consulted and proposed a large three-manual transept organ located at

gallery level with its own console in the gallery and a two-manual choir organ with its own console bracketed on the back wall of the apse above the choir stalls. The proposal to construct two independent organs was influenced by the fact that even though the transept and apse were adjoining, each functioned as a separate sound shell with its own acoustical environment requiring its own sound-producing sources. Holtkamp's ideas were enthusiastically approved, and the project was completed in 1951.

The Battell Chapel organ was Holtkamp's first major work in New England and did surprise some who were more familiar with Harrison's work at Aeolian-Skinner.

> Although installing a "classic style" Holtkamp at Yale in 1951 apparently caused a few ripples at the time, I must say that we never gave it a thought. We already had three Aeolian-Skinners and we felt it was time for a change of pace. Furthermore, we knew that Walter would be the ideal architect-builder for our purposes, and he was.[2]

The design of the Battell Chapel choir organ worked out so well that it became a model for certain other two-manual designs done later. Thus a comparison of the organ for the Chapel of Massachusetts Institute of Technology with the Yale instrument, both in visual as well as tonal design, reveals strong similarities. (See Appendix A.)

In 1952 Holtkamp demonstrated, again in Cleveland, that his talents were at their peak. The organ for St. Paul's Episcopal Church, Cleveland Heights, provided yet another opportunity for collaboration with Walter Blodgett, then organist-choirmaster at the church.[3] A new sanctuary had been erected, and Blodgett's "Babylonian Captivity" playing on a temporary installation of an electronic organ ended with the completion of the large three-manual instrument. The church, high and with splendid acoustics, had been planned for a Holtkamp to be located across the front of the sanctuary. The visual design, one of Holtkamp's most daring to date, became a pattern followed with minor revisions of detail in many later installations. In this sense, the St. Paul's Episcopal organ served the same catalytic function for later instruments as did the Cleveland Museum organ for the Oberlin and Syracuse installations.

With this instrument, as well as the large organ for Battell Chapel at Yale University, the tonal design stabilized into what can be called a standard Holtkamp stoplist. The major chorus reed now took its place on the Great, completing a process begun with the inclusion of reeds, but of less prominence, on the Greats of other major postwar instruments. The mechanical simplicity characteristic of most Holtkamps is also apparent at St. Paul's Episcopal with only one borrow in the entire organ (the Great Quintadena to Pedal) and the simple remote-location, toggle-switch combination action replacing the more complex remote, capture action of earlier large Holtkamps.[4]

The St. Paul's Episcopal organ can be taken as a good example of the mature style of Walter Holtkamp. It was perhaps his favorite instrument.[5] Many consider it to be his masterpiece. An examination of this instrument seems in order to help establish some of the characteristics of a typical Holtkamp organ of the mature period.

In a mature Holtkamp like St. Paul's, the important manual divisions are the Great and Positiv. The Great chorus is built upon a Principal 8' and the Positiv chorus is built upon a Principal 4', usually as powerful as, but of contrasting quality to, the Great Octave 4', and with a wooden Gedackt, called Copula, as its foundation. Contrast between these two divisions is achieved by their geographical separation in the organ layout and often, as at St. Paul's, by a difference of chest action and speech as well, i.e., a slider chest for one division (usually the Great) and a pitman chest for the other. The third manual division is enclosed and offers certain solo effects; a small reed chorus, and if large enough, as at St. Paul's Episcopal, a principal chorus much like a European Brustwerk in sound, and a pair of strings, usually of large scale and great breadth.[6] The Pedal division is very complete, with independent registers. In sound the Pedal is substantial enough to support almost the entire instrument without the use of manual to pedal couplers. The entire organ is placed in an open space within the room, with little or no casework in the European sense and no decorative pipe facade. The speaking pipes are arranged in a striking manner, usually with the smallest of each division located at the front of the chest.

These are the characteristics of a mature Holtkamp. But what of the sound? It seems big and aggressive. Perhaps it is this aggressive tutti which marks a Holtkamp organ more than any other single thing. Yet this bigness is deceptive, as Arthur Quimby perceptively observes. Clarity was Holtkamp's first goal and the grandeur and aggressiveness of sound was achieved more by suggestion rather than loudness per se.[7]

The Principals seem somewhat rough and dark in sound, especially in comparison with contemporary G. Donald Harrison instruments. With the addition of the Super Octave and the chorus mixture, the ensemble comes to life and all at once seems brilliant. The Great Principal Chorus, especially on the larger instruments, usually contained two mixtures, a Mixture IV, frequently breaking at every C, and a higher pitched Scharf III. Pipe scales normally include generously scaled trebles, with low cut up and sometimes with the upper lips a bit pulled out. In mixtures the quint ranks are almost equal in power to the unison ranks, although some are more gentle and with a higher cut up as well, especially in the Positiv Fourniture.

The flute registers are especially beautiful. "The large scaled metal gedackts are most similar to the classic stops of the seventeenth century, and have a warm, sombre, and velvety tone, with some speech attack in them."[8] The gedackts are voiced musically so that speech transients, while present, do not become an affectation, as was popular with other builders at that time. Most instruments have stopped or half-stopped flutes at 8' with the Positiv always of wood. The 4' flutes are usually metal stopped or half-stopped with the 4' Spitzflöte on the Great often more like a small principal than a flute. From time to time a wood stopped or half-stopped 4' flute would be used, especially if the 8' flute was of metal. The higher flutes and mutations are usually of large scale (the 2⅔' often stopped in the bass) and are voiced with character, yet with great care to assure a good blend with the lower gedackts, producing combinations of great color and power. The Pedal, when large enough, includes a Flute 4' which is often open and of very large scale, with small mouths producing a big, floating sound especially useful as a solo register.

The reeds are very European in sound.[9] They are often the least popular stops with some organists, yet the very criticisms raised, that they are buzzy and not loud enough, assure that the reeds blend well with the Principals and do not dominate the ensemble. The one exception to this practice is the Pedal Posaune, which is often huge and most assertive in a buzzy, rumbling, thoroughly delightful way, although not as useful as a more gentle reed might be. Many of the reeds utilize copper resonators, especially the Great and Pedal Trumpets and Posaune, and sometimes the Positiv Krummhorn, which is usually of half-length, relatively small in scale, and rather gentle in sound. Some Krummhorns have been used with wooden resonators, as have Dulzian registers, especially when specified for the

Great. The Swell 16' reed is usually cylindrical, covered and of half-length; the 8' a conical or double cone, full-length reed sometimes covered. The Swell 4' reed is usually conical and open. Often the Swell 8' reed is omitted on a smaller three-manual instrument to allow for reeds 16' and 4', the rationale being that the 8' is already present on the Great. Often the name on the console and the actual stop construction as given in a listing of organ registers with their "correct" construction does not agree.

The St. Paul's organ reflects Holtkamp's thinking about other facets of organ design. He never did like the tremulant and rarely included it in his instruments. The St. Paul's organ has none. (It also has no chimes!) By this time his tonal designs were complete in each division and only unison couplers were provided (at St. Paul's GP, SP, PP, SG, PG, SP). Occasionally Holtkamp would include a Swell to Pedal 4', especially if the instrument did not have a reed 4' in the Pedal. A few examples of the Positiv to Great 16' can be found, especially upon instruments designed for persons familiar with the Crouse organ, which includes such a coupler.

In keeping with his convictions about simplicity in design, Holtkamp avoided console gadgets as much as possible. He did provide a register crescendo pedal and a few reversibles (GP, SP, PP, Sfz) especially if requested by the organist, although for a time he discouraged inclusion of these devices.

As the decade of the fifties continued, the design and tonal ideals discussed above continued to be utilized. Towards the end of this period some of the visual designs became more daring and some (the Air Force Academy for one) were positively stunning. Often the tonal results seemed a bit less aggressive, more silvery than the instruments of the early fifties. Yet the basic design philosophy remained essentially constant, as may be observed by comparing the stoplists for Battell Chapel and St. Paul's Episcopal with the one for St. John's Abbey, Collegeville, Minnesota, which was the last large organ designed and completed by Walter Holtkamp before his death in 1962.

One of the unanswered questions about the work of Walter Holtkamp after the war was his gradual discarding of the slider chest and lack of interest in the then embryonic mechanical-action revival beginning in this country. In his talk, *Present-Day Trends*, he made clear that he held the strong opinion that the slider chest was best if one was to assure a good blend. On the basis of this talk and the strong article on the same subject written for the *American Organist* in 1938, it would have been reasonable to expect to see a move to the exclusive use of the slider chest soon after World War II. It also would have been reasonable to see some experimentation with mechanical action, especially in the light of the European trips of the early fifties. Yet these developments did not occur and Holtkamp gradually abandoned his interest in the slider chest, using it more rarely towards the end of the decade.

One can only speculate as to the reasons for this strange reversal on Holtkamp's part. Certainly one factor arguing against the further risks inherent in a move to tracker action was age. Many of his friends of the time, as well as Walter Holtkamp, Jr., agree in their speculation that he would have turned to tracker action if he had felt he was young enough. At age 56 (1950) one would think carefully before embarking on a new and somewhat risky course of action.

Another consideration arguing against further experimentation at this late date in his career was success. Finally, his work was generally accepted, and his place as one of the important American organ builders recognized even by those who did not personally appreciate his instruments. He had tried tracker action once before with the Portative of 1935 and had found little or no interest. In this context a scrap torn from a Cleveland Orchestra Program Book of the 1935-36 season, just at the time when his tracker experiment seemed doomed, becomes significant. The clipping was placed with other material gathered for use in his manuscript for a book on organ building, on which he worked extensively during the war. The program annotator writes of Brahms.

> The last of Brahms' four symphonies proclaims the autumn of the master's career, that final period which, extending from his third symphony to the end of his life, shows him definitely formed. As he advanced in years, he no longer sought to conquer new fields, but *devoted himself to the subtilization of familiar processes and the development of an ever higher degree of concentration.*[10]

The italics are Holtkamp's. Had he concluded that he had gone far enough and should perfect his art rather than experiment any further? Lawrence Phelps makes clear that his customers after the war did not seem interested in tracker instruments.[11] Such thoughts, coupled with his recognition after World War II, could provide strong arguments against risking success and reputation on a new venture.

Instead of a new direction, Holtkamp elected to continue in his now articulated style. He strongly defended his positions and argued against the need for organ cases, tracker action and slider chests. He let his well-voiced pipes in handsome exposed locations speak for themselves, and continued in his unique style of organ building.

Through his last decade of work, Holtkamp remained the leading exponent of free-standing, exposed organs. As Ochse observes, "Most organs were still being placed in chambers."[12] Even today, it is valid to observe that

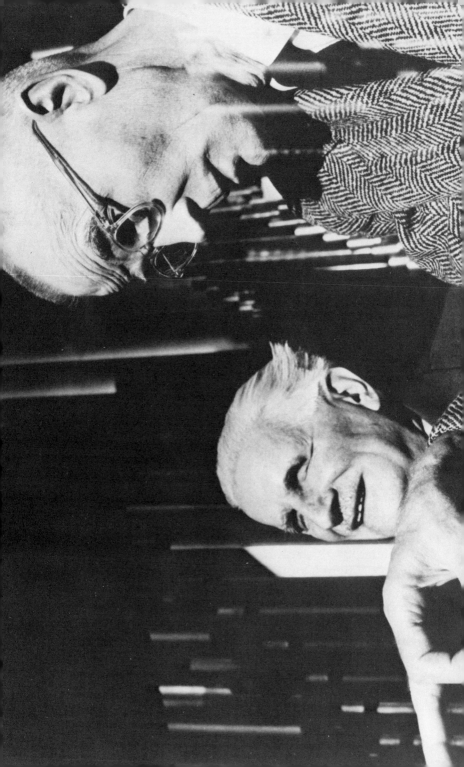

Holtkamp remains one of the few larger American firms that will not, for the sake of a contract, compromise the principle that an organ must be seen to be heard and agree to place an instrument in chambers.

Through his last decade Holtkamp also developed a stable style of stoplist, something not achieved with such consistency by any other American builder in this century. While details of scaling and voicing did vary because of the nature of the room and the organ's location in it, the instruments all behaved much in the same way. With the consoles so much alike and the quick responsiveness of the action, almost a Holtkamp trademark, the instruments seemed more consistently alike than those of other builders. A Holtkamp Great always had Principals 8', 4', 2' and at least a Mixture IV with, if large enough, Quintaton 16', Gedackt 8' and Spitzflöte 4'. The first cornet almost invariably appeared on the Positiv as an independent Nazard and Tierce, and the division usually had a Copula 8' as its only flue 8'. Such consistency of design was no accident.

> I am one who firmly believes that an organist should be able to go to a strange organ, and, after trying the effect of the instrument in the audience room, proceed to play with confidence and assurance, as do other instrumentalists. Allowances must of course be made for fine distinctions, as in other instruments and differences in builders, but in the main the effect of the various stops and the several divisions should be near enough alike so that the player feels at home on one organ as well as another.[13]

Holtkamp continued to eschew the large organ and for him an instrument of over 40 stops was a very large one. He maintained his interest in the small organ, and some very beautiful and successful small instruments came from the shop in this last decade. Early in his development Holtkamp had turned his back upon the unit organ as a solution to the problem of the small organ. With the exception of the Martini practice organ, designed for a rather special situation and in a way that avoided most of the pitfalls of a typical unit organ design, he remained true to this conviction against unification as a way to make an organ seem large and flexible. When prospective customers, pleased with the integrity and sound of his work, kept inquiring about a small organ, he agreed to build a one-manual instrument with a single pedal voice and manual to pedal coupler. This experiment proved successful, especially in the context of the design requirements, which asked for an instrument capable of leading the worship in a liturgical church of small membership. Over ten such instruments were produced, some with as many as three pedal stops and some subsequently enlarged by the addition of a second manual division. One such organ was constructed for the Lutheran Church of the Ascension (Birmingham, Michigan) in 1955.

Another small organ appeared in the mid-fifties and embodied so much of the essence of Holtkamp's style, convictions and interests, that it seems an appropriate instrument with which to conclude this chronological study of his work. The small organ of 12 stops for the Chapel of the Massachusetts Institute of Technology reveals Holtkamp, as much a radical in his field as Frank Lloyd Wright was in architecture, at work in a space designed by the respected contemporary architectural firm, Eero Saarinen and Associates. Here the combination of gifted organ builder working together with a creative architect demonstrates again that organ building, when practiced responsibly, can produce instruments of exceptional visual and aural distinction.

6

The Visual Dimension

No study of the work of Walter Holtkamp would be complete without mention of his unique abilities as a designer in the placing of pipes in free-standing, open positions. As late as the fifties, Holtkamp remained unequaled in America for his creativity in this field, while others have been, until more recently, very cautious in their approach to visual design.

Holtkamp's initial moves toward open placement, with installations like that in Brunnerdale Seminary, stemmed from his desire for clarity in sound. He became convinced early that direct, unobstructed access of sound from pipes to listener would result in a clearer sound, and also make possible the reduction of wind pressures in comparison to those necessary to get the sound of chambered pipes into the room in which they were to be heard. A quick discovery during these early experiments was that a set of pipes has a natural symmetry in shape, a phenomenon on which he capitalized in his designs.

Writing to architects in 1934, Holtkamp observed,

The most important consideration for the production of good organ tone is free and direct speech for the pipes. In general, it may be said that the organ should be given the same freedom of speech as the voice from the pulpit or choir. The musical value of an organ, or any instrument or group of instruments, including the human voice, is in direct proportion to its free standing position.[1]

With the installations of the Cleveland Museum Rückpositiv and the Covington organ, Holtkamp could put his developing ideas to work. Writing in the *American Organist*, Holtkamp defended his then radical ideas about the placement of the *entire* organ in a free-standing, open position. "It is my contention that organ chambers might more correctly be called organ containers, or possibly retainers, since they seem to bottle up the tone rather than allow it to be freely released."[2] He goes on to propose the idea that exposed pipes are an aesthetic asset to the organ rather than a liability to be endured for the sake of better tonal results. For him a creative arrangement of pipes could suggest "to the eye the counterpart of the massive and virile effect which the whole ensemble should produce."[3] He even defended the visible, moving swell-shutters. With shutters whose operation could be seen, "a feeling of expectancy is created similar to that in the orchestra when the brasses are poised for an entrance. If the swell-shutter is a legitimate apparatus for musical effects, has it not a right to be seen?"[4]

The organ at Covington, like many of the other early instruments, had quite extensive decoration of hand-carved wood surrounding the pipes. Many of the early designs are Gothic in style, possibly because the contour of pipes placed on an A-chest with the high point on a central axis tended to remind designers of Gothic possibilities. The fine wood carving necessary for such designs was readily at hand, which may have influenced the design in this direction as well.

In the early thirties, Holtkamp offered the use of floor space in his shop to a group of highly skilled woodworkers

forced out of work when a large Cleveland firm making church furnishings went bankrupt. Members of the group, calling themselves the Liturgical Arts Guild, worked in space in the factory and were available for advice, as well as for executing some of the beautiful designs that came from the shop in the thirties.[5]

As mentioned earlier, Holtkamp's visual designs were at first undertaken with the advice and assistance of architects and designers whom he knew and respected. It was only after World War II that he gained the confidence to undertake the sole responsibility for the visual design of his instruments. His work after the war is best known today and has been responsible for his reputation as a master of the art of visual design of instruments with exposed pipework. Phelps considers his work in this field to be without equal.[6] Yet his lesser-known work before the war, while not as spectacular as the later creations, may well be the more remarkable, especially in the context of the norm of the time, which was to place instruments in tonal tombs, euphemistically called chambers.

Blanton provides a good basic discussion of the early trends in placing organs in the open.

> The contemporary unencased organ came into being in the second decade of the 20th Century soon after the *Orgelbewegung* was launched. In its architectural treatment, it falls into four principal categories: the symmetrical functional, the asymmetrical functional, the symmetrical pipe-screen and the asymmetrical pipe-screen. There are, naturally, variants and combinations of these types, but they occur only rarely.
>
> The first category to be developed, the symmetrical functional, is that in which pipes are arranged about a center axis as symmetrically as is possible without resorting to pipes of false length, usually with the ranks of the smaller pipes in front. Although M-chests and, more often, A-chests may be used in these compositions, many pipes may be grouped arbitrarily to make the desired design.[7]

A study of Holtkamp's designs reveals three categories for his visual arrangements of pipes: symmetrical, asymmetrical, and unique, or one-time, solutions to a specific design problem not repeated or modified in a later instrument. Holtkamp's work follows Blanton's outline in that he first experimented with symmetrical arrangements of pipes, advancing to the asymmetrical forms only later as he gained confidence in his ability. Holktamp tended to avoid pipe-screens although portions of certain instruments (Fairmount Presbyterian Church, Cleveland, and St. John's Roman Catholic Cathedral, Cleveland, to cite two), did utilize pipe-screens for portions of the instruments.

The symmetrical designs tended to place the Great in the center of the instrument, usually upon A-chest or modified A-chest, with the Swell behind and usually raised above the level of the Great chest. The Pedal pipes were placed at the sides of the instrument depending upon space and number of pipes to arrange. The organs at Covington and Miles Park Presbyterian and the main portion of the Baldwin Wallace instrument provide examples of this approach to the arrangement of the organ. The presence of a third manual division presented problems for this design approach, unless the Positiv could become a Rückpositiv. At Baldwin Wallace the Positiv was placed at the opposite side of the narrow stage from the main organ, thus providing for the spatial separation of the Great and Positiv in a low room, which prevented the more usual arrangement to achieve this separation.

The organ in St. Paul's Lutheran, Cleveland, which Blanton considers to be one of the most beautiful visually of all the Holtkamp organs, solves the problem of the third manual division with a Rückpositiv.[8] The pipes of the Rückpositiv stand completely in the open, which contrasts with the main organ, where pipes of the Pedal and Quintaton provide what is almost a screen for the other three divisions. The pipes in the central tower are from the Pedal Quint with the Principal 16' of wood back in the organ. The carving of composers' names across the base of the case, and the angles playing on their trumpets at the corners of the Rückpositiv, provide other examples of the work made possible through the skilled wood craftsmen in the Holtkamp shop. The symbols of the seasons and feast days in the church year, painted in color on shields placed on the oak casework, hark back to the painted details on the Our Lady of Peace organ, possibly the only other instrument made by Holtkamp with such a wealth of detail in its casework. The St. Paul's Lutheran instrument, with its symmetrical Rückpositiv and a main case with pipes arranged asymmetrically within a symmetrical housing, stands at a transition point in Holtkamp's designs. His interest in the potential of asymmetrical arrangements of pipes was beginning to take precedence over the earlier symmetrical practice.

Holtkamp's move to a more asymmetrical pipe arrangement may well have been precipitated partially by his concern for an arrangement of the two open manual divisions spatially separated from each other. To date he had constructed few three-manual instruments, so the problem of the third manual division had not clashed with his symmetrical approach. When he did execute a three-manual organ before World War II, it was usually in a gallery situation that permitted a Rückpositiv, the perfect solution musically as well as aesthetically. Now with his increasing acceptance as an organ builder, he was being asked to place instruments in locations other than a gallery, locations that did not allow for a Rückpositiv.

His first solution to these problems was that adapted for the Cleveland Museum and then expanded for Warner

Hall, Oberlin College, and Crouse Hall, Syracuse University. Here, as discussed in an earlier chapter, the Positiv was placed at the organist's left side, balanced by Pedal upperwork from Principal 8' on the right. The Great was placed in the center with the Swell behind and above. This design approach remains essentially a modification of the original symmetrical two-manual organs with Great and Swell on the central axis and large chests for Positiv and Pedal at the front of the sides, and at Oberlin and Syracuse at right angles to the chests of the Great and Swell. Again the large Pedal pipes are disposed around the sides with a tower of a few low pipes of the Pedal Principal placed directly behind the Great and asymmetrically to the right of the design's central axis to emphasize the height of these instruments, tie the lines of the high Swell together with the lower Great, and provide a dramatic asymmetrical accent to the essentially symmetrical nature of the design.

The organ at St. Paul's Episcopal, Cleveland Heights, provides an early example of the asymmetrical approach to organ design that was to be the norm for most instruments in the last decade of Holtkamp's work. The Great remains in the center, in this instrument upon a slider chest of LC design. The Positiv is placed to the left and at a slight angle, with the Swell directly behind and above. The large Pedal pipes are placed against the rear wall at the extreme left with the main chest for the Pedal being a C-chest at left front with the tallest pipes in the rear.

This basic design, with some modifications to meet a given situation, was repeated many times over. Thus even in his layout of instruments, Holtkamp could be true to his earlier stated premise that organs should be enough alike that the player feels at home on one as well as another. Anyone who has played upon many Holtkamps realizes the truth of this assertion, since usually things seem to

Cantate ei canticum novum:
bene psallite ei in vociferatione.

Oratio spiritu, oratio...
psallam spiritu, psallam...

come from the same general location in relation to the console, Great in center, Positiv to the right, etc.

While adopting a consistent approach to the layout of his instruments, Holtkamp did provide many creative solutions to specific physical environments that did not provide for one of his more normal design concepts. The Air Force Academy design, completed late in his career, is one well-known example of his brilliance and mastery of the free-standing, open approach to organ design. Another is the organ at Concordia Seminary, St. Louis.

> As three-dimensional design, the Holtkamp organ in Concordia Lutheran Seminary, St. Louis, Missouri, is truly a work of art. Although strictly contemporary in concept, it has as much architectonic quality as do the cases of Gothic and early Renaissance times. Natural rakes of pipe ranks on an M-chest, an A-chest with a chromatic chest are used knowingly with overhangs, cantilevers, plane surfaces and a twisted support to gain an enviable result. The well-executed inscriptions are the only extraneous decoration indulged in, for even the stopper grips of the topmost pipes, which give a helpful accent of color, are functional.[9]

Thus the visual dimension of Walter Holtkamp's art has developed. His work with the unencased, free-standing organ is probably unique in the world, and now, with the advent of interest in the encased organ, may well remain unequalled.

7
Epilog

Walter Holtkamp in his speech, *Present-Day Trends in Organ Building*, provided the student of his work with a clear statement of his philosophy of organ building. It is significant to note, with the exception of his abandoning of the slider chest, how true to his philosophy, evolved in the thirties, he was to be in his mature instruments. Two other convictions, not mentioned in *Present-Day Trends*, also have disciplined and influenced his work. As he often mentioned in other talks and articles, he was interested in smaller organs and wished to evolve an American style of organ building.

Holtkamp did not like large organs. Writing in the *American Lutheran* in 1933, he articulated this dimension of his philosophy.

> The watchword should be smaller organs, of finer quality, in advantageous positions. They are more of a pleasure to build and certainly more of a pleasure to listen to.[1]

Perhaps his small shop with its spirit of trust and pride in high quality work reinforced this dimension of his design philosophy. With a small firm, he was under little pressure to produce large instruments or compromise his standards in order to keep his men busy. Holtkamp affirmed simplicity in his instruments and did not trust complex, mechanical gadgetry. He often observed that his instruments should be as simple as a haywagon. His small firm did not have the resources for much experimentation with complicated mechanical equipment, and therefore the smaller and simpler organ became a result not only of conviction but necessity. The modest size of the company also assured that Holtkamp could keep personal control and supervision over the many details involved in the construction of an organ. In fact, he may well have been the only major organ builder in the country, especially until the founding in the early sixties of new smaller firms, to consistently demand and have such total control over the location, placement, design, construction and installation of his instruments.

In addition to an aversion to large, complex organs, a study of Holtkamp's talks and articles documents his conviction that he was building instruments for America, instruments which were not copies of European organs, hence the title of this study, *Walter Holtkamp, American Organ Builder*. As early as a 1932 talk to the Cleveland A.G.O. chapter, he spoke of his concern for an American organ for American rooms, typically less resonant than their European counterparts. While affirming that the American organs of the early twentieth century were "a sin against good taste," he cautioned against the mere copying of any specific style of European organ.

> We Americans must get back to first principles, forget our fancy solo stops and develop an American organ to suit our own conditions. Europe can be used as a storehouse for information. Europe can help in our organ education just as she helps in the education of our doctors, architects, painters, etc., but she cannot be our model.[2]

Leonard Raver relates an interesting story in this regard. He

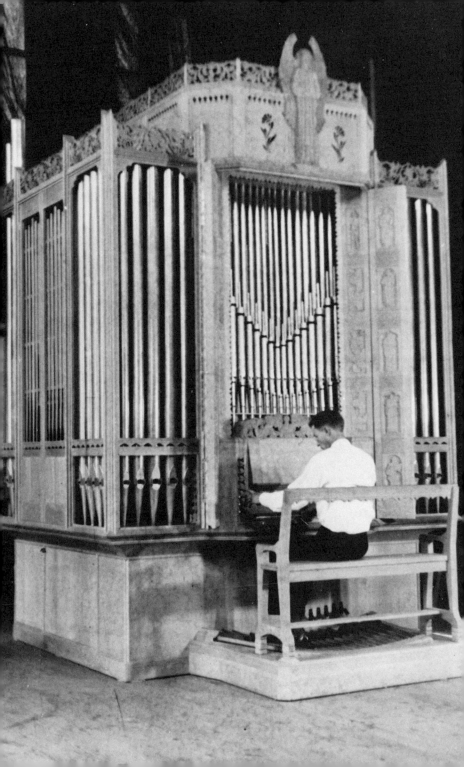

had played the opening recital on the Corpus Christi Organ in New York and was about to leave for European study. Holtkamp, who had come to New York for the recital, heard of Raver's plans and warned him to remember that he was an American and to come back an American. "We don't need to be converted," was his admonition.[3]

Walter Holtkamp's organs are American. Conceived for the less reverberant environments which are typical in this country, and able to meet the wide variety of musical demands made upon them, his instruments are eclectic in design, reflecting America's eclectic cultural lifestyle. Yet they are not, for example, mere combinations of a French Reed Chorus with English Diapason Chorus. They are new creations influenced and informed by the lessons of the past, and leavened by an understanding of their place and use in contemporary America.

Holtkamp believed that if an instrument was basically musical and had integrity of design and construction, it could provide a suitable vehicle for the performance of a reasonable range of organ literature. "My theory of organ building or my philosophy of organ building is to design instruments which will play the greatest possible range of existing literature of the organ, and make this music clear and meaningful to the audience in the auditorium."[4] The all-purpose organ was the goal of both G. Donald Harrrison and Walter Holtkamp although, as Phelps points out, "Holtkamp was willing to work in a much smaller frame."[5]

In attempting to achieve his all-purpose organ, Holtkamp, through his more limited approach and his insistence upon very open positions for his instruments, was probably more consistently successful than Harrison. In the process he also evolved a style of organ building, both tonally and visually, that remains unique. Few builders in America have been as successful in evolving a style of organ building and remaining true to it when subjected to the many pressures acting to modify and even to corrupt it. Few have had as significant an influence for good upon the whole history of organ building in this country. And very few have produced instruments of such unique design and importance that their name has become a legend.

Notes

1. Walter Holtkamp (1894-1962)

1. Unless otherwise cited, biographical information on the Holtkamp family is based on my conversations with Walter Holtkamp, Jr., and the records in the company archives.
2. Unless otherwise cited, information on the firm, now called the Holtkamp Organ Company, is from the company archives.
3. Orpha Ochse, *The History of the Organ in the United States* (Bloomington: Indiana University Press, 1975), pp. 324–27.
4. William H. Barnes, *The Contemporary American Organ*, 6th ed. (New York: J. Fischer & Bro., 1956), p. 81.
5. Ibid., p. 78.
6. Walter Holtkamp, Jr., interview, Cleveland, Ohio, 6 May 1975.
7. Ochse, *History of the Organ*, p. 349.
8. Joseph Sittler, "A Biographical Sketch of Walter Holtkamp's Evolving Tonal Philosophy." Holtkamp archives.
9. F. R. Webber, "A Holtkamp Story," *The Diapason* 53 (April 1962): 28.
10. Grigg Fountain to John Ferguson, Evanston, Illinois, 15 July 1975.
11. Holtkamp, Jr., interview.
12. John Fesperman, *Two Essays on Organ Design* (Raleigh: Sunbury Press, 1975), Prologue, p. xiii.
13. Lawrence I. Phelps, *A Short History of the Organ Revival* (St. Louis: Concordia Publishing House, 1967), p. 14.
14. Walter Holtkamp, Address to Chicago Chapter, American Guild of Organists, 1939.
15. Walter Holtkamp, "Organ Music and Organ Architecture," *Architecture* (June 1934): 356.
16. Charles McManis to John Ferguson, Kansas City, Kansas, 10 August 1975.
17. Arthur Poister, transcript of interview, Kent, Ohio, 9 November 1973.
18. Fesperman, *Two Essays*, p. 63.

19. Finn Videro to John Ferguson, Copenhagen, Denmark, 5 April 1978.
20. Holtkamp, Jr., interview.
21. Fenner Douglass to John Ferguson, Wellfleet, Massachusetts, 9 June 1975.
22. Dick Flentrop to John Ferguson, Zaandam, Netherlands, 7 April 1978.

2. Years of Transition (1931-1933)

1. For discussions of pipe arrangements, I will employ the terminology utilized by Joseph Blanton in *The Organ in Church Design* (Albany, Texas: Venture Press, 1957). On pp. 72–73 Blanton makes a distinction between unenclosed ("stops which are outside swell boxes even though they may be located within an organ case or an organ chamber or behind an organ screen") and unencased ("pipes which are wholly outside an organ case and which are within the church interior"). Blanton also utilizes the letters "A" and "M" to describe the visual effect of chests with pipes arranged with the tallest pipes at the central axis of the chest (A) and with the tallest pipes alternating chromatically at each side of the chest, the shortest in the center (M). To these descriptions I will add the letter "C" to represent a chromatic chest with all the tallest pipes placed at one side (RC—tallest pipes at right; LC—tallest pipes at left).
2. All dates given are from the factory records and have been checked for accuracy whenever possible. There is some confusion in other sources over the installation dates of certain instruments (Blanton errs on Covington by 6 years) as well as other dates mentioned in the narrative. The author hopes to help clear up this confusion and has tried to be most cautious when claiming "firsts." It is remarkable how information can become so confused only a few years removed from time of occurrence.
3. Another sentence in the second letter, 30 March 1932, gives a hint of that dogmatism for which Holtkamp was justifiably famous. Responding to a complaint that the Salicional was too soft in the bottom range, Holtkamp promises to come to Brunnerdale to check it. "If, considering your remarks in regard to this particular register, *I* find that it can stand bringing out some more, we will of course be very glad to do so" [italics mine].
4. Phelps, *Short History*, p. 3.
5. Arthur J. Thompson, "Some Reflections on Organ Ensemble," *The Diapason* 18 (March 1927): 40.
6. Sittler, *Biographical Sketch*.
7. Ibid.
8. Sir Henry Deterding, as told to Stanley Naylor, "An International Oilman," *Saturday Evening Post*, 23 September 1933, p. 5.
9. Webber, "Holtkamp Story," p. 28.

3. Radical Years (1933-1945)

1. Sittler, *Biographical Sketch*.

2. Martha Smith to Walter Holtkamp, Jr., Cambridge, Massachusetts, 25 May 1975.

3. Sittler, *Biographical Sketch*.

4. Carleton H. Bullis, "New Rueckpositiv on Cleveland Organ Is First in America," *The Diapason* 25 (December 1933): 11.

5. Blanton, *Organ in Church*, p. 355.

6. Walter Holtkamp, "An Organ to See and Hear," *The American Organist* 18 (July 1934): 269.

7. Walter Blodgett, transcript of interview, Cleveland Museum of Art, 18 June 1973.

8. The book mentioned is *Die Entwicklungsgeschichte der Orgelbaukunst* (Einsiedeln: Benziger, 1929).

9. Holtkamp, "An Organ to See," p. 272.

10. Sittler, *Biographical Sketch*.

11. Ochse, *History of the Organ*, p. 411, pp. 414–17.

12. Fenner Douglass relates an amusing story about the trouble one Portative had in finding a home. It seems that one had been purchased for a convent in Cleveland but upon delivery was received with extreme displeasure by the nuns. When Holtkamp heard their complaints he responded by offering $50 to buy it back. The furious nuns agreed, Holtkamp removed the organ and promptly offered it to Quimby for the $50. The same instrument subsequently appeared in concert in New York's Town Hall. The final chapter in the story of the unloved Portative occurred years later and is contributed by Walter Holtkamp, Jr., who upon an offer from Quimby purchased the instrument, again for $50, refurbished it, and donated it to the Cleveland Museum of Art.

13. Sittler, *Biographical Sketch*.

14. Blodgett, interview.

15. In a letter dated 23 October 1974, written as a follow-up of our earlier long interview, a transcript of which Blodgett had recently reviewed, he commented about his personal likes in mixtures in his usual delightful prose. "My point about having mixtures of different strength as well as pitch composition has always fallen on turned off ears. They are always of equally loud intensity, requiring strong under support to justify turning on the brilliance. That is why I have always asked for a Dolce Cornet in the Swell so I could have some mixture flavor in a moderate dynamic. I know the inclusion of a tierce rank is naughty according to the omniscient books. I join Nero Wolfe in saying pfui."

16. Joseph Bonnet to Walter Holtkamp, New York, 5 March 1942.

17. Sittler, *Biographical Sketch*.

18. Blodgett, interview.

19. Walter Holtkamp, "Present-Day Trends in Organ Building," *Proceedings of the Music Teachers National Association* 1940, p. 396.

20. Ibid., p. 398.

21. Ibid., p. 399.

22. Ibid., p. 400.

23. Ibid.
24. Ibid., p. 401.
25. Ibid., p. 402.
26. Ibid.

4. Towards a Mature Style (1945-1950)

1. Walter Blodgett, *Notes for Inaugural Concert, McMyler Memorial Organ* (Cleveland: Cleveland Museum of Art, 1971), p. 4.
2. The interest of the Kulas family, now continued through the Kulas Foundation, in providing organs for Cleveland institutions is well known. Significant Holtkamp organs given by Kulas include the Baldwin Wallace instrument, completed in 1942, and the Cleveland Institute of Music instrument, completed in 1972, as well as the gift to the Cleveland Museum of Art, which precipitated the important 1946 rebuild of the McMyler Memorial Organ.
3. Blodgett, *Notes*, p. 5.
4. Albert Schweitzer to Walter Holtkamp, Günsbach, Alsace, 22 May 1934. The letter, in Schweitzer's handwriting, was accompanied by the translation quoted in the text provided at his request by a member of his hospital staff with him on his European trip.
5. Blodgett, *Notes*, p. 5.
6. *Cleveland Plain Dealer*, 13 July 1949.
7. Blodgett, *Notes*, p. 6.
8. Poister, interview.
9. Fountain, letter.
10. Ibid. The Warner Hall discussed is the concert hall in the original Conservatory building, destroyed in 1965 to make room for the new King building.
11. Poister, interview.
12. Fountain, letter.
13. Ibid. Other prominent names in American organ building whose experience includes time in the Holtkamp shop include Charles Fisk, Charles McManis, and Robert Noehren.

5. Mature Years (1950-1962)

1. Fesperman, *Two Essays*, p. 56.
2. Luther Noss to John Ferguson, New Haven, Connecticut, 20 February 1978.
3. The collaboration of Blodgett and Holtkamp is quite remarkable, especially in length of time and variety of instruments involved. With the 1936 Positiv at St. James' Church as the first, Blodgett was involved as consultant or resident organist in at least seven organs in the Cleveland area alone.
4. While Holtkamp did provide a remote capture combination action if requested, especially if the instrument was large and to be used in a teaching situation, it is clear that he preferred his more simple and troublefree remote toggle-switch action, which was little more than a perfected setterboard system as had been used for years, especially in theatre organs.

5. While sources differ as to which instruments remained favorites of Walter Holtkamp throughout his lifetime, the following are consistently mentioned by most and are listed in order of construction: Our Lady of the Angels, Cleveland, 1942; Crouse Hall, Syracuse, 1950, and St. Paul's Episcopal, Cleveland Heights, 1952. The Cleveland Museum organ was also a special favorite primarily because the Museum was the site of his first triumph with the Rückpositiv as well as because of the long association with Curator Walter Blodgett, who encouraged and allowed much tonal experimentation on the instrument. The organs at Yale University Battell Chapel, 1951, and University of California, Berkeley, Hertz Memorial Hall, 1958, were also favorites, perhaps because they represented his acceptance as an organ builder by these distinguished institutions that were so much a part of the cultural establishment from which he had so long been divorced.

6. While Holtkamp often labeled the Swell mixture Plein Jeu, the stop was usually designed so that a high cymbel mixture resulted. The Plein Jeu at St. Paul's is not typical in that it is rather low in pitch, a reflection of the desires of Blodgett, who also specified the Aeoline 4 and Dolce Cornet for the Swell. Holtkamp often included a Sesquialtera in the Swell but he considered the stop to be a rather big sound. Blodgett wished a very gentle sound and the factory records of this stoplist emphasize this point with a dark underlining of the word "Dolce." See also note 15, Chapter III.

7. Arthur Quimby to John Ferguson, Plainfield, New Hampshire, 18 July 1975.

8. Eugene M. Nye, "Walter Holtkamp—A Master Organ Builder," *The Organ* LI (October 1971): 75.

9. The European sound of Holtkamp reeds is partially explained by the fact that the firm has utilized reeds from Giesecke and Sohn, Göttingen, Germany, almost exclusively, beginning with the reeds obtained for the Warner Hall rebuild.

10. Cleveland Orchestra Program Book, 1935-36 Season.

11. Phelps, *Short History*, p. 15.

12. Ochse, *History of the Organ*, p. 409.

13. Walter Holtkamp, manuscript for a book on organ building.

6. The Visual Dimension

1. Holtkamp, "Organ Music," p. 355.

2. Holtkamp, "Organ to See and Hear," p. 270.

3. Ibid.

4. Ibid., p. 272.

5. Webber, "Holtkamp Story," pp. 28–29.

6. Phelps, *Short History*, p. 11.

7. Blanton, *Organ in Church*, p. 355. See also note 1, Chapter II.

8. Ibid., p. 372.

9. Ibid., pp. 375–76.

7. Epilog

1. Walter Holtkamp, "The Modern Organ," *American Lutheran* XVI (March 1933): 11.
2. Walter Holtkamp, Address to Cleveland Chapter, American Guild of Organists, 1932.
3. Leonard Raver to John Ferguson, New York, 14 May 1978.
4. Holtkamp, Chicago Address.
5. Phelps, *Short History*, p. 14.

APPENDIX A

Stoplists of Significant Instruments Discussed in the Text

I. **Detroit Society of the New Church, Detroit, Michigan**

Job Number 1557, 1930

Great 5" Wind
8   DIAPASON
8   Gamba (Choir)
8   Melodia (Choir)
4   Octave Gamba (Choir Gamba)
4   Flute Harmonic (Choir)
2   FIFTEENTH
8   TUBA
     CHIMES

Swell 6" Wind
16   LIEBLICH FLUTE
8   VIOLIN DIAPASON
8   GEDECKT
8   Flute Dolce (Lieblich 16)
8   SALICIONAL
8   VOIX CELESTE
8   AEOLINE
4   VIOLINA
4   Flute Amabile (Lieblich 16)
2-2/3   Twelfth (Lieblich 16)
2   Flageolet (Lieblich 16)

8 CORNOPEAN
8 ORCHESTRAL OBOE
8 VOX HUMANA

Choir 4" Wind
8 GAMBA
8 LUDWIG TONE
8 MELODIA
8 GEMSHORN
4 FLUTE HARMONIC
8 CLARINET

Pedal
16 CONTRA BASS
16 BOURDON
16 Lieblich Gedackt (Swell)
10-2/3 Quint (Swell 16)
8 Flute (Bourdon 16)
8 Dolce Flute (Swell 16)
5-1/3 Octave Quint (Swell 16)
4 Octave Flute (Swell 16)
2-2/3 Super Octave Quint (Swell 16)

II. **All Saints Episcopal Church, Minot, North Dakota**

Job Number 1563, 1931

Great 4" Wind
16 Tenor Gedackt (Swell 8)
8 OPEN DIAPASON
8 DULCIANA
8 LUDWIGTONE
8 Gedackt (Swell 8)
4 Flute d'Amour (Swell 8)
4 Seraphtone (Ludwigtone 8)
2 Flautino (Swell 8)
   CHIMES
   HARP

Swell 6" Wind
8   GEIGEN PRINCIPAL
8   STOPPED DIAPASON
8   VIOLIN
8   VOIX CELESTE
8   ECHO CHOIR
8   Ludwigtone (Great)
4   Flute (Swell 8)
2   Seraphspfeife (Great Ludwigtone)
    Tremolo

Pedal 4" Wind
16 SUB BASS
16 Bourdon (Swell 8)
8   Pedal Bass (Swell 8)
4   Choral Bass (Swell 8)

III.   **Brunnerdale Seminary, Canton, Ohio**

Job Number 1571, 1932

entire organ enclosed except Great Diapason, Principal and Pedal Bourdon

Great 3" Wind
8   OPEN DIAPASON
4   PRINCIPAL
8   Rohr Flute (Swell)
8   Gamba (Swell)
4   Flute d'Amour (Swell Rohr Flute)
4   Fugara (Swell Gamba)
2-2/3   Twelfth (Swell Rohr Flute)
2   Fifteenth (Swell Gamba)

Swell 5" Wind
16 SALICIONAL
8   ROHR FLUTE (wood-drilled stoppers)
8   GAMBA
8   LUDWIGTONE
4   Fugara (Gamba)

    4   Flute d'Amour (Rohr Flute)
2-2/3   Twelfth (Rohr Flute)
    2   Fifteenth (Gamba)
    8   REED

        Pedal 3" Wind
   16   BOURDON
   16   Contra Salicional (Swell)
    8   Cello (Swell Gamba)
    8   Octave (Swell Rohr Flute)
    4   Flute (Swell Rohr Flute)

IV. **St. John's Lutheran Church, Cleveland, Ohio**

Job Number 1573, 1932

entire organ enclosed except Great principals

        Great 3" Wind
    8   DIAPASON
    4   PRINCIPAL
        II MIXTURE
    8   VIOLA DOLCE
    8   Rohr Floete (Swell)
    4   Flute d'Amour (Swell 8)

        Swell 5" Wind
    8   ROHR FLOETE (wood-drilled stoppers)
    8   LUDWIGTONE
    4   GEMSHORN
    4   Flute d'Amour (Rohr Flute)
2-2/3   NACHTHORN
    2   OCTAVA (wood-harmonic)
    8   TRUMPET AMABILE

        Pedal 3" Wind
   16   BOURDON
   16   Contra Viola (Great Viola)
    8   Gedeckt (Swell Rohr Flute)

8   Cello (Great Viola)
4   Super Octave (Great Viola)
4   Flute (Swell Rohr Flute)

Mixture Composition

Note 1	20	25
Pitch 2	2-2/3	2-2/3
1	2	2
	1	

V.   Cleveland Museum of Art, Cleveland, Ohio

Job Number 1580, 1933

Rückpositiv

8   BOURDON (wood)
4   PRESTANT (copper)
4   ROHRFLÖTE (37 pipes; 25-61)
2-2/3 NAZARD (1-24 chimney; 25-61 taper)
2   GEMSHORN
1-3/5 TIERCE
1-1/3 LARIGOT (24 pipes; 1-24)
1   PICCOLO (24 pipes; 1-24)
       III FOURNITURE

Fourniture Composition

Note 1	13	25	37
Pitch 1	1-1/3	2	4
2/3	1	1-1/3	2-2/3
1/2	2/3	1	2

VI.   St. John's Roman Catholic Church, Covington, Kentucky

Job Number 1581, 1934

Great 2-3/4" Wind notes 1-27
4" Wind notes 28-68

16 QUINTATON
8 DIAPASON
8 SALICIONAL
8 LUDWIGTONE
4 PRESTANT (copper)

Swell 3-1/2" Wind notes 1-27
　　　　4" Wind notes 28-61
8 HARMONIC FLUTE
8 GAMBA
4 GEMSHORN
2-2/3 NAZARD
1-3/5 TIERCE
III—V MIXTURE
4 OBOE CLARION

Pedal 3-1/2" Wind
16 CONTRA BASS (open wood)
16 Quintaton (Great)
8 CELLO (4" Wind)
8 POSAUNE (4" Wind)

Mixture Composition

Note 1	25	43	50
Pitch 2	2-2/3	4	5-1/3
1	2	2-2/3	4
	1-1/3	2	2-2/3
	1	1-1/3	2
		1	

VII.　**Miles Park Presbyterian Church, Cleveland, Ohio**

Job Number 1583, 1934

Great 3" Wind
16 LIEBLICH GEDECKT (metal)
8 DIAPASON
8 SALICIONAL

```
 4   PRINCIPAL
 4   ROHR FLÖTE
```

Swell 4" Wind

```
 8     VIOLIN DIAPASON
 8     FLUTE HARMONIC
 8     AEOLINE
 4     FLUTE (open wood)
2-2/3  NAZARD
1-3/5  TIERCE
       IV PLEIN JEU
 8     CROMORNE
 4     OBOE CLARION
```

Pedal 3" Wind
Reeds - 5" Wind

```
16   SUBBASS
16   Lieblich Gedackt (Great)
 8   QUINTATON
 4   GEMSHORN
16   POSAUNE
 8   FAGOTTO
```

Plein Jeu Composition

Note	1	18	25	30	37
Pitch	2	2	2	2-2/3	4
	1-1/3	1-1/3	2	2	2-2/3
	1	1	1-1/3	2	2
	1/2	2/3	1	1-1/3	2

VIII.   **St. James' Episcopal Church, Cleveland, Ohio**

Job Number 1596 (Positiv), 1936,
1602 (Great, Swell, Pedal new console), 1937

Great 3-1/2" Wind

```
16    QUINTATON
 8    PRINCIPAL
 8    GEDECKT
5-1/3 GROSS QUINT
```

Swell 3-1/2″ Wind
8 FLUTE (harmonic)
8 GAMBE
4 GEIGEN
IV KORNET MIXTURE
8 FAGOTTO

Positiv 2-1/2″ Wind
8 QUINTATON (metal)
4 PRESTANT (copper)
III-IV CYMBAL

Pedal 3-1/2″ Wind
16 SUBBASS
16 Quintaton (Great)
8 OCTAVE
4 CHORAL BASS
16 DULZIAN

Mixture Compositions

Swell IV Kornet

Note	1	13	25	37
Pitch	2	2	4	4
	1-1/3	1-3/5	2	2-2/3
	1	1-1/3	1-3/5	2
	3/5	1	1-1/3	1-3/5

Positiv III-IV CYMBAL (small case)

Note	1	18	25	37
Pitch	2	2	2	2-2/3
	1-1/3	1-1/3	1-3/5	2
	1/2	1	1	1-3/5

Note: At a later date the Great 5-1/3 was moved to 4 and the 1-3/5 in the Positiv Cymbal silenced.

IX. **Emmanuel Lutheran Church, Rochester, New York**

Job Number 1598, 1937

      Great 3" Wind
8 PRINCIPAL
4 NACHTHORN

      Swell 3" Wind
8 QUINTATON (metal)
4 PRESTANT
    IV-III MIXTURE

      Pedal 3" Wind
16 SOUBASSE
4 CHORAL BASSE

    Couplers

Great to Pedal 8
Great to Pedal 5-1/3
Great to Pedal 4
Swell to Pedal 8
Swell to Swell 16
Swell to Great 16
Swell to Great 8
Great to Great 4

Mixture Composition

Note	*1*	*25*	*27*	*49*
Pitch	2	2	2-2/3	3-1/5
	1-1/3	1-3/5	2	2-2/3
	1	1-1/3	1-3/5	2
	3/5			

X. **Baldwin-Wallace College, Berea, Ohio**

Job Number 1611, 1942

      Great 3" Wind
16 QUINTATON

```
   8  PRINCIPAL
   8  COPULA
   4  OCTAVE
   4  SPITZFLÖTE
2-2/3  QUINTE
   2  SUPER OCTAVE
      IV MIXTURE
```

Swell 3-1/2" Wind
```
   8  HARMONIC FLUTE
   8  GAMBA
   8  VOIX CELESTE
   4  FLUTE (open wood)
   2  PICCOLO (stopped wood)
      III DOLCE CORNET
         (2-2/3, 2, 1-3/5)
      V PLEIN JEU
   8  TROMPETTE
   4  OBOE
```

Positiv 2-1/2" Wind
```
   8  QUINTATON (metal)
   4  PRINCIPAL
   4  ROHRFLÖTE
2-2/3  NAZARD
   2  OCTAVA
1-3/5  TIERCE
      III FOURNITURE
```

Pedal 4" Wind
```
  16  SUBBASS
  16  Quintaton (Great)
   8  ROHR GEDACKT
   4  CHORAL BASS
  16  DULZIAN
   8  FAGOTT
   4  CROMORNE
```

Mixture Compositions

Great IV Mixture

Note	1	13	25	37
Pitch	2	2-2/3	4	5-1/3
	1-1/3	2	2-2/3	4
	1	1-1/3	2	2-2/3
	2/3	1	1-1/3	2

Swell V Plein Jeu

Note	1	18	25	32	37	44
Pitch	2-2/3	4	4	4	8	8
	2	2-2/3	2-2/3	2-2/3	4	4
	1-1/3	2	2	2	2-2/3	4
	1	1-1/3	1-1/3	2	2-2/3	2-2/3
	2/3	1	1-1/3	1-1/3	2	2

Positiv III Fourniture

Note	1	13	25	37
Pitch	1	1-1/3	2	4
	2/3	1	1-1/3	2-2/3
	1/2	2/3	1	2

XI. Our Lady of the Angels Roman Catholic Church, Cleveland, Ohio

Job Number 1614, 1942

Entire organ on 3-1/2" Wind

Great

16	QUINTADEN
8	PRINCIPAL
8	COPULA
8	SPITZFLÖTE
4	OCTAVE
4	ROHRFLÖTE
	IV MIXTURE

Swell

8 BOURDON
4 GEMSHORN
2 NACHTHORN
V PLEIN JEU
8 CHROMORNE
4 OBOE CLARION

Rückpositiv

8 SINGENDE GEDACKT
4 ROHRFLÖTE
2-2/3 NAZARD
2 OCTAVA
II SESQUIALTERA (2-2/3–1-3/5)

Pedal

16 SUBBASS
16 Quintaton (Great)
8 OCTAVE
8 FLAUTO DOLCE
4 CHORAL BASS
8 POSAUNE

Additions, 1951

Great

2-2/3 NAZARD
2 DOUBLETTE
8 TRUMPET

Pedal

III MIXTURE (2-2/3–2-1)
16 POSAUNE
4 SCHALMEY

Mixture Compositions

Great IV Mixture (1941)

Note	1	37	49
Pitch	2-2/3	4	5-1/3
	2	2-2/3	4
	1-1/3	2	2-2/3
	1	1-1/3	2

Great IV Mixture (1951)

Note	1	13	25	37	49
Pitch	1-1/3	2	2-2/3	4	5-1/3
	1	1-1/3	2	2-2/3	4
	2/3	1	1-1/3	2	2-2/3
	1/2	2/3	1	1-1/3	2

Swell V Plein Jeu

Note	1	13	25	30	37	49
Pitch	2	2	4	4	8	8
	1-1/3	1-3/5	2	2-2/3	4	4
	1	1-1/3	1-3/5	2	2-2/3	3-1/5
	3/5	1	1-1/3	1-3/5	2	2-2/3
	1/2	1/2	1/2	1-1/3	1-3/5	2

XII. **Draft Stoplist, An Ideal Small Three Manual Organ**

Joseph Bonnet—Summer 1942, with Walter Blodgett and Walter Holtkamp

Great
16 QUINTADENA
8 PRINCIPAL
8 GEDACKT
8 FLUTE
4 OCTAVE
4 NACHTHORN
2-2/3 QUINTE

2 DOUBLETTE
IV MIXTURE
8 CROMORNE

Swell
8 GAMBE
8 VOIX CELESTE II
8 GEDACKT
4 PRINCIPAL
4 BOURDON
2 DOUBLETTE
III CORNET
V PLEIN JEU
8 SCHALMEY
4 OBOE CLARION

Positiv
8 QUINTATON
4 PRINCIPAL
4 ROHRFLÖTE
2-2/3 NAZARD
2 QUARTE
1-3/5 TIERCE
III CYMBAL

Pedal
32 SUBBASS
16 BOURDON
16 Quintadena (Great)
8 FLUTE
8 GEDACKT
4 CHORALBASS
III MIXTURE
16 POSAUNE
8 TRUMPET
4 ZINK

Walter Holtkamp, American Organ Builder

XIII. **First Unitarian Church, Cleveland, Ohio**

Job Number 1619, 1943

Rebuild of 1904 Möller. Upon closing of the church, removed and installed in Maryville College Chapel, Maryville, Tennessee

	Great 3" Wind
16	QUINTADENA
8	PRINCIPAL
8	FLUTE
8	QUINTATON
4	OCTAVE
4	NACHTHORN
2-2/3	QUINTE
2	SUPER OCTAVE
	IV FOURNITURE
8	CROMORNE

	Swell 3" Wind
8	VIOLA
8	GEDACKT
8	VOIX CELESTE (II)
8	AEOLINE
4	OCTAVE
4	BOURDON
2	FLAUTINO
	III CORNET (2-2/3–2–1-3/5)
	IV MIXTURE
8	FAGOTT

	Rückpositiv 3" Wind
8	COPULA
4	PRINCIPAL
4	ROHRFLÖTE
2-2/3	NAZARD
2	DOUBLETTE
1-3/5	TIERCE
	III CYMBALE

Pedal 3-1/2" Wind

32	CONTRABASS (to low E, C to D# quints)
16	SUBBASS
16	Quintadena (Great)
8	OCTAVE
8	FLAUTO DOLCE
5-1/3	QUINTE
4	CHORAL BASS
2	OCTAVA
	II TERZIAN (3-1/5–2-2/3)
16	POSAUNE
8	TRUMPET

Mixture Compositions

Great VI Fourniture

Note	1	13	25	37
Pitch	2	2-2/3	4	5-1/3
	1-1/3	2	2-2/3	4
	1	1-1/3	2	2-2/3
	2/3	1	1-1/3	2

Swell IV Mixture

Note	1	13	25	37	49
Pitch	2	2	4	4	4
	1-1/3	1-3/5	2	2-2/3	3-1/5
	1	1-1/3	1-3/5	2	2-2/3
	3/5	1	1-1/3	1-3/5	2

Positiv III Cymbale

Note	1	13	20	30	37	44	54
Pitch	2	2	2	4	4	8	8
	1	1	1-1/3	2	2-2/3	4	5-1/3
	1/2	2/3	1	1-1/3	2	2-2/3	4
						2	2-2/3

XIV.   **Cleveland Museum of Art, Cleveland, Ohio**

Job Number 1524, 1946

Rebuild of 1922 E. M. Skinner

      Great
- 16 QUINTADENA
- 8 PRINCIPAL
- 8 GEDACKT
- 8 SALICIONAL
- 4 FIRST OCTAVE
- 4 SECOND OCTAVE
- 4 SPITZFLÖTE
- 2-2/3 QUINTE
- 2 SUPER OCTAVE
- IV MIXTURE
- IV HARMONICS
- 16 DULZIAN
- 8 SCHALMEY

      Positiv (1933 reused)
- 8 COPULA
- 4 PRINCIPAL
- 4 ROHRFLÖTE
- 2-2/3 NAZARD
- 2 DOUBLETTE
- 1-3/5 TIERCE
- III FOURNITURE

      Choir
- 8 CONCERT FLUTE
- 8 DULCIANA
- 8 ERZAHLER CELESTE II
- 4 FUGARA
- 2 FLAUTINO
- 8 FLUGEL HORN

Swell

8	GEIGEN PRINCIPAL
8	FLUTE A' CHIMINEE
8	GAMBA
8	GAMBA CELESTE
8	QUINTATON
4	OCTAVE GEIGEN
4	BOURDON
2	OCTAVLEIN
2	BLOCKFLÖTE
	III DOLCE CORNET (2-2/3–2–1-3/5)
	V PLEIN JEU
16	CONTRA FAGOTT
8	TROMPETTE
8	VOX HUMANA
4	CLARION

Pedal

32	CONTRABASS
16	MAJOR BASS (open wood)
16	Subbass (Contrabass)
16	Quintedena (Great)
16	LIEBLICH GEDACKT
8	OCTAVE
8	GEMSHORN
8	GEDACKT
5-1/3	QUINTE (stopped)
4	CHORAL BASS
4	NACHTHORN (stopped)
2	PICCOLO
	III MIXTURE (2-2/3–2–1-1/3)
16	POSAUNE
16	Dulzian (Great)
8	TRUMPET
4	CROMORNE

Mixture Compositions

Great IV Mixture

Note	1	13	25	37	49
Pitch	1-1/3	2	2-2/3	4	5-1/3
	1	1-1/3	2	2-2/3	4
	2/3	1	1-1/3	2	2-2/3
	1/2	2/3	1	1-1/3	2

Great IV Harmonics (retained from Skinner)

Swell V Plein Jeu

Note	1	20	32	44
Pitch	2-2/3	4	5-1/3	8
	2	2-2/3	4	5-1/3
	1-1/3	2	2-2/3	4
	1	1-1/3	2	2-2/3
	2/3	1	1-1/3	2

Positiv III Fourniture (as in 1933)

XV. St. Paul's Lutheran Church, Cleveland, Ohio

Job Number 1636, 1949

Consultants: Walter Blodgett and Grigg Fountain. Included some pipes (marked +) from earlier instrument.

Great 3-1/2'' Wind
16 QUINTADENA
8 PRINCIPAL
8 GEDACKT
4 OCTAVE +
4 SPITZFLÖTE
2-2/3 QUINTE +
2 SUPER OCTAVE +
IV MIXTURE
8 KRUMMHORN (6'' Wind)

Swell 5" Wind

8 GEIGEN PRINCIPAL
8 BOURDON +
8 QUINTATON
8 VOIX CELESTE II +
4 OCTAVE GEIGEN +
4 FLUTE +
2 BLOCKFLÖTE +
   III DOLCE CORNET (2-2/3–2–1-3/5)
   V PLEIN JEU
8 TROMPETTE
4 OBOE CLARION

Rückpositiv 3-1/2" Wind

8 COPULA
4 PRINCIPAL
4 ROHRFLÖTE
2-2/3 NAZARD
2 DOUBLETTE
1-3/5 TIERCE
   III FOURNITURE

Pedal 3-1/2" Wind

16 CONTRA BASS + (wood)
16 SUB BASS +
16 LIEBLICH GEDACKT +
16 Quintadena (Great)
10-2/3 GROSS QUINTE (metal)
8 OCTAVE +
8 VIOLONE +
8 Flauto Dolce (Lieblich)
4 CHORAL BASS
4 Flute + (Lieblich)
   III MIXTURE (2-2/3–2–1-1/3)
16 POSAUNE (6" Wind)
8 Trumpet (Posaune)
8 Krummhorn (Great)
4 Krummhorn (Great)

Mixture Compositions

Great IV Mixture

Note	1	13	25	37	49
Pitch	1-1/3	2	2-2/3	4	5-1/3
	1	1-1/3	2	2-2/3	4
	2/3	1	1-1/3	2	2-2/3
	1/2	2/3	1	1-1/3	2

Swell V Plein Jeu

Note	1	20	32	44
Pitch	1-2/3	4	4	8
	2	2-2/3	4	4
	1-1/3	2	2-2/3	4
	1	1-1/3	2	2-2/3
	2/3	1	1-1/3	2

Positiv III Fourniture

Note	1	13	25	37	49
Pitch	1	1-1/3	2	2-2/3	4
	2/3	1	1-1/3	2	2-2/3
	1/2	2/3	1	1-1/3	2

XVI. Practice Organ—Oberlin College, Oberlin, Ohio

Job Number 1641, 1949

Pedal
16 GEDACKT
8 GEDACKT
4 PRINCIPAL
4 QUINTADENA

Lower Manual
8 GEDACKT
4 PRINCIPAL
4 QUINTADENA
II CYMBEL

Upper Manual

8	QUINTADENA (low 12 Gedackt)
4	GEDACKT
2	PRINCIPAL
1-1/3	LARIGOT (Gedackt)

ANALYSIS 3" Wind

16–8–4–1-1/3	GEDACKT (wood)		97 pipes
4	PRINCIPAL		73 pipes
4	QUINTADENA		61 pipes
	II CYMBEL		122 pipes

Note	1	13	25	37	55
Pitch	2/3	1	1-1/3	2	2-2/3
	1/2	2/3	1	1-1/3	2

After the first four practice instruments were built, the Pedal was revised by extending the QUINTATON down to replace the GEDACKT 16. The mixture was revised to break at each octave.

XVII. **Syracuse University—Crouse Hall, Syracuse, New York**

Job Number 1649, 1950

Included pipes from Roosevelt-Estey in Crouse Hall and Aeolian in Hendricks Chapel. Because this instrument still exists unchanged in its original installation and considering its importance, derivations from earlier organs are given.

Great 3" Wind

16	QUINTADENA
8	PRINCIPAL
8	GEDACKT C Swell Stopped Diapason 8
8	GEMSHORN C Great Gemshorn 8
4	GROSSOCTAV C Choir Geigen 8
4	OCTAVE
4	STIPZFLÖTE
2-2/3	QUINTE

```
   2  SUPER OCTAVE
      IV MIXTURE
      III SCHARF
  16  DULZIAN
   8  SCHALMEY


      Swell 4-1/2" Wind
  16  LIEBLICH GEDACKT C Swell Lieblich 16
   8  GEIGEN PRINCIPAL
   8  ROHRFLÖTE
   8  GAMBA C Swell Salicional 8
   8  CELESTE C Swell Celeste 8
   8  FLAUTO DOLCE
   8  FLUTE CELESTE
   4  OCTAVE GEIGEN C Swell Octave 4
   4  BOURDON C Great Flute d'Amour 4
         (wood-drilled stoppers)
   2  FLAUTINO C Swell Flageolet 2
 1-1/3 LARIGOT
      II SESQUIALTERA C Swell Cornet
      V PLEIN JEU
  16  BASSOON
   8  TROMPETTE
   8  OBOE
   4  CLARION


      Positiv 4-1/2" Wind
   8  COPULA
   8  QUINTADENA C Choir Quintaton 8
   4  PRINCIPAL
   4  ROHRFLÖTE
 2-2/3 NAZARD
   2  DOUBLETTE
   2  NACHTHORN
 1-3/5 TIERCE
   1  SIFFLÖTE
      III CYMBEL
   8  CROMORNE
```

Pedal (8' Flues and up on one chest 4-1/2" Wind;
   balance on 4-1/2" or higher)

32	Grand Bourdon 12 pipe extention with chest from H
16	PRINCIPAL C Pedal Diapason 16 (metal)
16	SUBBASS C Pedal Bourdon 16
16	GAMBA H Pedal Violone 16 (wood)
16	Quintadena (Great)
16	Lieblich Gedackt (Swell)
8	OCTAVE C Great Diapason II 8
8	VIOLONE C Swell Spitzflöte 8
8	STILLE GEDACKT
5-1/3	QUINTE C Swell Diapason 8
4	CHORALBASS C Great Octave 4
4	HOHLFLÖTE C Swell Hohlflöte 4
2	PICCOLO
	II RAUSCHQUINTE C Great Quinte 2-2/3 plus new 2
	III MIXTURE (2–1-1/3–1) C Great Mixture
16	POSAUNE C Pedal Trombone 16
16	Dulzian (Great)
8	TRUMPET C Swell Cornopean
4	ROHR SCHALMEY
2	Rohr Schalmey (Rohr Schalmey)

Mixture Compositions

Great IV Mixture

Note	1	13	25	37	49
Pitch	1-1/3	2	2-2/3	4	5-1/3
	1	1-1/3	2	2-2/3	4
	2/3	1	1-1/3	2	2-2/3
	1/2	2/3	1	1-1/3	2

Great III Scharf

Note	1	9	17	25	33	41	49
Pitch	1/2	2/3	1	1-1/3	2	2-2/3	4
	1/3	1/2	2/3	1	1-1/3	2	2-2/3
	1/4	1/3	1/2	2/3	1	1-1/3	2

Swell V Plein Jeu

Note	1	13	25	37	49	54
Pitch	2	2	2-2/3	4	5-1/3	8
	1	1-1/3	2	2-2/3	4	5-1/3
	2/3	1	1-1/3	2	2-2/3	4
	1/2	2/3	1	1-1/3	2	2-2/3
	1/3	1/2	2/3	1	1-1/3	2

Positiv III Cymbel

Note	1	13	25	37	49
Pitch	1	1-1/3	2	2-2/3	4
	2/3	1	1-1/3	2	2-2/3
	1/2	2/3	1	1-1/3	2

XVIII. **Yale Univesity, Battell Chapel, New Haven, Connecticut**

Job Number 1653, 1951

Great 3" Wind
16 QUINTADENA
 8 PRINCIPAL
 8 GEDACKT
 4 OCTAVE
 4 SPITZFLÖTE
2-2/3 QUINTE
 2 SUPER OCTAVE
    IV MIXTURE
    III SCHARF
16 DULZIAN
 8 TRUMPET

Swell 3-1/2" Wind
 8 GEIGEN PRINCIPAL
 8 ROHRFLÖTE
 8 GEMSHORN
 8 GEMSHORN CELESTE
 4 OCTAVE GEIGEN

4   GEDACKT
2   FLAUTINO
1-1/3   LARIGOT
    II SESQUIALTERA (2-2/3–1-3/5)
    IV PLEIN JEU
16   BASSON
8   FAGOTT
4   ROHR SCHALMEY

Rückpositiv 3-1/2″ Wind
8   COPULA
4   PRINCIPAL
4   ROHRFLÖTE
2-2/3   NAZARD
2   DOUBLETTE
    III FOURNITURE
8   CROMORNE

Pedal 3-1/2″ Wind
16   PRINCIPAL
16   SUBBASS
16   Quintadena (Great)
8   OCTAVE
8   BOURDON DOLCE
4   CHORALBASS
4   HOHLFLÖTE
2   NACHTHRON
    III MIXTURE (2–1-1/3–1)
16   POSAUNE
16   Dulzian (Great)
8   TRUMPET
4   Clarion (Trumpet)
2   CORNET

Apse Great 3-1/2″ Wind
8   GEDACKT
4   PRINCIPAL
4   SPITZFLÖTE
1-1/3   LARIGOT

Apse Positiv 3-1/2" Wind

8 QUINTADENA
4 ROHRFLÖTE
2 PRINCIPAL
II CYMBAL

Apse Pedal 3-1/2" Wind

16 QUINTADENA
8 GEDACKT POMMER
4 CHORALBASS

Mixture Compositons

Great IV Mixture

Note	1	13	25	37	49
Pitch	1-1/3	2	2-2/3	4	5-1/3
	1	1-1/3	2	2-2/3	4
	2/3	1	1-1/3	2	2-2/3
	1/2	2/3	1	1-1/3	2

Great III Scharf

Note	1	9	17	25	33	41	44
Pitch	1/2	2/3	1	1-1/3	2	2-2/3	4
	1/3	1/2	2/3	1	1-1/3	2	2-2/3
	1/4	1/3	1/2	2/3	1	1-1/3	2

Swell IV Plein Jeu

Note	1	13	25	37	49
Pitch	2	2	2-2/3	4	8
	1	1-1/3	2	2-2/3	4
	2/3	1	1-1/3	2	2-2/3
	1/2	2/3	1	1-1/3	2

Positiv III Fourniture

Note	1	13	25	37	49
Pitch	1	1-1/3	2	2-2/3	4
	2/3	1	1-1/3	2	2-2/3
	1/2	2/3	1	1-1/3	2

Apse Positiv II Cymbal

Note	1	13	25	37	55
Pitch	2/3	1	1-1/3	2	2-2/3
	1/2	2/3	1	1-1/3	2

XIX. St. Paul's Episcopal Church, Cleveland, Ohio

Job Number 1657, 1952

Great 3″ Wind
- 16 QUINTADENA
- 8 PRINCIPAL
- 8 FLUTE
- 8 GEDACKT
- 4 OCTAVE
- 4 SPITZFLÖTE
- 2-2/3 QUINTE
- 2 SUPER OCTAVE
- IV MIXTURE
- III SCHARF
- 8 TRUMPET

Swell 3″ Wind
- 8 ROHRFLÖTE
- 8 LIEBLICH GEDACKT
- 8 GAMBA
- 8 GAMBA CELESTE
- 4 OCTAVE GEIGEN
- 4 BOURDON
- 4 AEOLINE
- 2 FLAUTINO

```
        III DOLCE CORNET (2-2/3–2–1-3/5)
        IV PLEIN JEU
 16     BASSON
  8     FAGOTT
  4     ROHR SCHALMEY
```

Positiv 3″ Wind

```
  8     COPULA
  4     PRAESTANT
  4     ROHRFLÖTE
2-2/3   NAZARD
  2     DOUBLETTE
1-3/5   TIERCE
        III FOURNITURE
  8     CROMORNE
```

Pedal 3″ Wind

```
 32     POLYPHONE (upper 24 from Subbass)
 16     PRINCIPAL
 16     SUBBASS
 16     Quintadena (Great)
  8     OCTAVE
  8     GEDACKT
  4     CHORAL BASS
  4     NACHTHORN
        III MIXTURE (2-2/3–2–1-1/3)
 32     CORNET
 16     Cornet
 16     POSAUNE
  8     TRUMPET
  4     SCHALMEY
```

Mixture Compositions

Great IV Mixture

Note	1	13	25	37	49
Pitch	1-1/3	2	2-2/3	4	8
	1	1-1/3	2	2-2/3	4
	2/3	1	1-1/3	2	2-2/3
	1/2	2/3	1	1-1/3	2

Great III Scharf

Note	1	9	17	25	33	41	49
Pitch	1/2	2/3	1	1-1/3	2	2-2/3	4
	1/3	1/2	2/3	1	1-1/3	2	2-2/3
	1/4	1/3	1/2	2/3	1	1-1/3	2

Swell IV Plein Jeu

Note	1	13	25	37	49
Pitch	2	2	2-2/3	4	8
	1	1-1/3	2	2-2/3	4
	2/3	1	1-1/3	2	2-2/3
	1/2	2/3	1	1-1/3	2

Positiv III Fourniture

Note	1	13	25	37	49
Pitch	1	1-1/3	2	2-2/3	4
	2/3	1	1-1/3	2	2-2/3
	1/2	2/3	1	1-1/3	2

Pedal Cornet Composition

32 CORNET

Lowest Note Pipe Length	Approximate Sounding Pitch	Derivation
16	C	Principal
10-2/3	G	Subbass
8	C	Octave
6-2/5	E	independent rank
5-1/3	G	Subbass
4-4/7	A#	independent rank
4	C	Choral Bass
3-1/2	D	independent rank
2-3/4	F#	independent rank
2-1/2	G#	independent rank

16 CORNET

Lowest Note Pipe Length	Derivation	Lowest Note Pipe Length	Derivation
8	Octave	2-2/7	extention 4-4/7
5-1/3	Subbass	2	Great Flute 8
4	Choral Bass	1-3/4	extention 3-1/2
3-1/5	extention 6-2/5	1-3/8	extention 2-3/4
2-2/3	Great Flute 8	1-1/4	extention 2-1/2

XX. Massachusetts Institute of Technology Chapel, Cambridge, Massachusetts

Job Number 1674, 1955

Great 2-7/8" Wind
8 COPULA
8 DULCIANA
4 PRINCIPAL
2 HOHLFLÖTE
   III MIXTURE

Pedal 2-7/8" Wind
16 QUINTADENA
8 GEDACKT
4 CHORAL BASS

Positiv 2-7/8" Wind
8 QUINTATON
4 ROHRFLÖTE
2 PRINCIPAL
   II CYMBEL

Mixture Compositions

Great III Mixture

Note	1	13	25	37	49
Pitch	1	1-1/3	2	2-2/3	4
	2/3	1	1-1/3	2	2-2/3
	1/2	1/2	1	1-1/3	2

Positiv II Cymbel

Note	1	17	33	41
Pitch	2/3	1	1-1/3	2
	1/2	2/3	1	1-1/3

XXI. St. John's Abbey, Collegeville, Minnesota

Job Number 1742, 1961

Great 2-3/4" Wind
- 16 QUINTADENA
- 8 PRINCIPAL
- 8 FLUTE
- 8 GEDACKT
- 4 OCTAVE
- 4 SPITZFLÖTE
- 2 SUPER OCTAVE
- 1-1/3 OCTAVE QUINTE
- IV MIXTURE
- III SCHARF
- 8 TRUMPET

Swell 2-3/4" Wind
- 8 ROHRFLÖTE
- 8 LIEBLICH GEDACKT
- 8 SPITZGAMBE
- 8 VOIX CELESTE
- 4 OCTAVE GEIGEN
- 4 BOURDON
- 2 DOUBLETTE
- 1 PICCOLO
- II SESQUIALTERA
- IV PLEIN JEU
- 16 BASSON
- 8 FAGOTT
- 4 OBOE CLARION

Positiv 2-3/4″ Wind

8	COPULA
4	PRAESTANT
4	ROHRFLÖTE
2-2/3	NAZARD
2	OCTAVIN
2	BLOCKFLÖTE
1-3/5	TIERCE
	III FOURNITURE
8	CROMORNE

Pedal 2-3/4″ Wind

16	PRINCIPAL
16	SUBBASS
16	Quintaton (Great)
10-2/3	QUINTBASS
8	OCTAVE
8	FLAUTO DOLCE
4	CHORALBASS
4	NACHTHORN
	IV MIXTURE (2–1-1/3–1-2/3)
32	CORNET (see Job 1657)
16	POSAUNE
8	TRUMPET
4	SCHALMEY

Mixture Compositions

Great IV Mixture

Note	1	13	25	37	49
Pitch	1-1/3	2	2-2/3	4	4
	1	1-1/3	2	2-2/3	2-2/3
	2/3	1	1-1/3	2	2-2/3
	1/2	2/3	1	1-1/3	2

Great III Scharf

Note	1	9	17	25	33	41	49
Pitch	1/2	2/3	1	1-1/3	2	2-2/3	4
	1/3	1/2	2/3	1	1-1/3	2	2-2/3
	1/4	1/3	1/2	2/3	1	1-1/3	2

Swell IV Plein Jeu

Note	1	13	25	37	49	55
Pitch	1	1-1/3	2	2-2/3	4	4
	2/3	1	1-1/3	2	2-2/3	2-2/3
	1/2	2/3	1	1-1/3	2	2-2/3
	1/3	1/2	2/3	1	1-1/3	2

Positiv III Fourniture

Note	1	16	23	28	47	52
Pitch	2/3	1	1-1/3	2	2-2/3	4
	1/2	2/3	1	1-1/3	2	2-2/3
	1/3	1/2	2/3	1	1-1/3	2

A Chronological List of Instruments by Walter Holtkamp

The material for this list is taken from the factory archives. The dates given are for year of completion of the instrument. Absence of a date indicates that, although designed, the instrument was never constructed. The table provides the job number, location and name of institution as well as date of completion.

Job Number	Institution	Date
1566	Cleveland, Ohio Messiah Lutheran Church	1931
1567	Cleveland, Ohio Kaufmann Funeral Home	1931
1568	Cleveland, Ohio Phillips Avenue Presbyterian Church	1931
1569	Cleveland, Ohio John Carroll University	
1570	Cleveland, Ohio St. James Church	
1571	Canton, Ohio Brunnerdale Seminary	1932
1572	Saginaw, Michigan Ames Methodist Episcopal Church	1932
1573	Cleveland, Ohio St. John's Lutheran Church	1932

Job Number	Institution	Date
1574	Cleveland, Ohio St. Vitus Roman Catholic Church	1932
1575	Dover, Ohio St. John's Evangelical Church	1938
1576	Detroit, Michigan Zion Lutheran Church	1932
1577	Pompano, Florida H. P. Robinson—Residence	1932
1578	Cleveland, Ohio Our Lady of Peace Roman Catholic Church	1933
1579	Cleveland, Ohio St. Stanislaus Roman Catholic Church	1933
1580	Cleveland, Ohio Cleveland Museum of Art	1933
1581	Covington, Kentucky St. John's Roman Catholic Church	1934
1582	Cleveland, Ohio St. Margaret Roman Catholic Church	1934
1583	Cleveland, Ohio Miles Park Presbyterian Church	1934
1584	Unknown	
1585	Portative #1	1935
1586	Cleveland, Ohio Bethany Lutheran Church—Parma	
1587	Portative #3 Walter Holtkamp Residence	1935
1588	Macedonia, Ohio Hawthornden State Hospital	1935
1589	Cleveland, Ohio Christ Church	
1590	Cleveland, Ohio First Unitarian Church	
1591	Cleveland, Ohio Brooklyn Masonic Temple	

Job Number	Institution	Date
1592	Cleveland, Ohio	
	Sisters of the Holy Ghost Convent	
1593	Lorain, Ohio	1935
	St. Stanislaus Roman Catholic Church	
1594	Millersville, Ohio	1936
	St. Mary's Roman Catholic Church	
1595	Pine Mountain, Kentucky	1936
	Pine Mountain Settlement School	
1596	Cleveland, Ohio	1936
	St. James Episcopal Church	
1597	Cleveland, Ohio	
	St. James Episcopal Church	
1598	Rochester, New York	1937
	Emmanuel Lutheran Church	
1599	Cleveland, Ohio	1936
	St. Philomena Roman Catholic Church	
1600	La Grange, Illinois	1937
	First Congregational Church	
1601	Cleveland, Ohio	1937
	St. Stephen's Roman Catholic Church	
1602	Cleveland, Ohio	1937
	St. James Episcopal Church	
1603	Pemberton, New Jersey	1938
	Grace Episcopal Church	
1604	La Salle, Illinois	1938
	First Congregational Church	
1605	Bloomington, Indiana	1939
	University of Indiana	
1606	Cleveland, Ohio	1938
	Hawken School Chapel	
1607	Not built as yet	
1608	Nashville, Tennessee	1940
	Fisk University	
1609	Evanston, Illinois	1940
	First Presbyterian Church	
1610	Cleveland, Ohio	1940
	St. Mary's Roman Catholic Church	

Job Number	Institution	Date
1611	Berea, Ohio Baldwin-Wallace College	1942
1612	Cleveland, Ohio Fairmount Presbyterian Church	1942
1613	Olivet, Michigan Olivet College	1942
1614	Cleveland, Ohio Our Lady of the Angels Roman Catholic Church	1942
1615	Cleveland, Ohio St. Cecelia's Roman Catholic Church	1942
1616	Cleveland, Ohio St. Clements Roman Catholic Church	1942
1617	Cleveland, Ohio St. Vincent de Paul Roman Catholic Church	1942
1618	Cleveland, Ohio Holy Name Roman Catholic Church	1942
1619	Cleveland, Ohio First Unitarian Church	1943
1620	Cleveland, Ohio Euclid Avenue Temple (Rebuild)	1944
1621	Kent, Ohio First Congregational Church (Rebuild)	1944
1622	Delaware, Ohio Ohio Wesleyan University	1945
1623	Georgetown, Kentucky First Presbyterian Church	1945
1624	Cleveland, Ohio Cleveland Museum of Art	1946
1625	Cleveland, Ohio Fairmount Presbyterian Church Chapel	1946
1626	Ashtabula, Ohio St. Peters Episcopal Church	1946
1627	Cleveland Heights, Ohio First Church of Christ Scientist	1947
1628	Struthers, Ohio St. Nicholas Roman Catholic Church	1946

Job Number	Institution		Date
1629	Saginaw, Michigan St. James Lutheran Church		
1630	Cleveland, Ohio St. Johns Cathedral—Gallery		1948
1631	Cleveland, Ohio St. Johns Cathedral—Chancel		1948
1632	Not built as yet		
1633	Cleveland, Ohio St. Malachi Roman Catholic Church		
1634	Chagrin Falls, Ohio The Federated Church		
1635	Cleveland, Ohio St. Mary's Seminary		
1636	Cleveland, Ohio St. Paul's Lutheran Church—East 55th Street		1949
1637	Lexington, Kentucky Christ Church Episcopal		1949
1638	Ypsilanti, Michigan St. Luke's Church		1949
1639	Kenosha, Wisconsin Kempor Hall		1949
1640	Elyria, Ohio First Congregational Church		1949
1641	Oberlin, Ohio Oberlin College—Practice Organ		1949
1642	San Antonio, Texas Trinity Universalist Church		1949
1643	Coraeopolis, Pennsylvania St. Joseph's Roman Catholic Church		1949
1644	Naugatuck, Connecticut St. Michael's Episcopal Church		1950
1645	Williamstown, Massachusetts E. B. Stube—Residence		1954
1646	Oberlin, Ohio Warner Hall	1950,	51, 52
1647	Dunkirk, New York St. John's Church		1959

Job Number	Institution	Date
1648	San Antonio, Texas First Church Christ Scientist	
1649	Syracuse, New York Syracuse University—Crouse Hall	1950
1650	Syracuse, New York Syracuse University—Practice Organ	1950
1651	Louisville, Kentucky Woman's Missionary Training School	1951
1652	Paris, Kentucky St. Peters Episcopal Church	1951
1653	New Haven, Connecticut Yale University—Battell Chapel	1951
1654	Maryville, Tennessee Maryville College—Practice Organ	1951
1655	Maryville, Tennessee Maryville College—Concert Organ	1951
1656	San Antonio, Texas Don Willing—Residence	1951
1657	Cleveland Heights, Ohio St. Paul's Episcopal Church	1952
1658	Syracuse, New York Syracuse University—Practice Organ (removed and re-installed at Meredith College, Raleigh, North Carolina)	1952
1659	Syracuse, New York Syracuse University—Hendricks Chapel	1952
1660	Lexington, Kentucky University of Kentucky	1952
1661	Wooster, Ohio Wooster College	1953
1662	St. Louis, Missouri Concordia Seminary	1953
1663	Honolulu, Hawaii Atherton Memorial Chapel	1953
1664	New York, New York Julliard School of Music	1952

Job Number	Institution	Date
1665	River Forest, Illinois Concordia Teachers College	1953
1666	Houghton, New York Houghton College	1953
1667	Culver City, California Grace Lutheran Church	1953
1668	Cleveland, Ohio Blessed Sacrament Church	1953
1669	Cleveland, Ohio Epworth Euclid Methodist Church	1954
1670	Grand Island, Nebraska Trinity Lutheran Church	1954 1966
1671	Houston, Texas Trinity Lutheran Church	1954
1672	Middletown, Delaware St. Andrews School	1954
1673	Maryville, Tennessee Maryville College Chapel	1957
1674	Cambridge, Massachusetts M.I.T. Chapel	1955
1675	Cleveland, Ohio—Parma St. Charles Roman Catholic Church	1955
1676	Goldsboro, North Carolina St. Stephen's Church	1955
1677	Wellesley, Massachusetts Wellesley College—Positiv	1955
1678	Park Forest, Illinois Hope Lutheran Church	1954
1679	Birmingham, Michigan Church of the Ascension (Lutheran)	1955
1680	Cambridge, Massachusetts M.I.T. Auditorium	1956
1681	Toledo, Ohio Collingwood Presbyterian Church	1956
1682	Evanston, Illinois Northwestern University	1955

Job Number	Institution	Date
1683	Marysville, Michigan Pilgrim Lutheran Church	1955
1684	Princeton, New Jersey William Scheide—Residence	1956
1685	Tuscaloosa, Alabama University of Alabama—Practice Organ	1955
1686	Yardley, Pennsylvania Church of the Resurrection (Lutheran)	1956
1687	Des Moines, Iowa University Christian Church	1956
1688	San Fernando, California Chapel of the Cross	1956
1689	Cambridge, Massachusetts Episcopal Theological School	1956
1690	Affton, Missouri Lutheran Church of the Reformation	1957
1691	Kent, Connecticut Kent School	1956
1692	New York, New York Corpus Christi Roman Catholic Church	1956
1693	Palos Heights, Illinois Church of the Good Shepherd	1956 1964
1694	Rome, Georgia Shorter College	1957
1695	Cincinnati, Ohio Christ Church	1957
1696	Des Plaines, Illinois Immanuel Lutheran Church	
1697	Milwaukee, Wisconsin Church of the Cross	1957
1698	Syracuse, New York Syracuse University—Practice Organ	1956
1699	Berkeley, California University of California	1958
1700	Moorhead, Minnesota Trinity Lutheran Church	1957

Walter Holtkamp, American Organ Builder

Job Number	Institution	Date
1701	Grosse Pointe, Michigan Christ Church	1958
1702	Indianapolis, Indiana Pilgrim Lutheran Church	1957
1703	Ames, Iowa Memorial Lutheran Church	1957
1704	Hartford, Connecticut Trinity Episcopal Church	1958
1705	Macon, Georgia Holy Trinity Lutheran Church	1957
1706	Hollins College, Virginia Hollins College	1959
1707	Middletown, Ohio Church of the Ascension	1959
1708	Grosse Pointe, Michigan Christ Church—Choir Room–Practice Organ	1958
1709	Hollins College, Virginia Hollins College—Meditation Chapel	1959
1710	New Haven, Connecticut Yale University—Practice Organ	1958
1711	Cleveland, Ohio St. Mary's of Assumption Church	1957
1712	New York, New York General Theological Seminary	1958
1713	Cleveland, Ohio Holy Cross Lutheran Church	1958
1714	Toledo, Ohio Good Shepherd Lutheran Church (removed and re-installed in Lutheran Student Chapel, Bowling Green, Ohio)	1958 1969
1715	Atlanta, Georgia Lutheran Church of the Ascension	1958
1716	Amherst, Massachusetts Amherst College	1959
1717	Berkeley, California University of California—Practice Organ	1959

Job Number	Institution	Date
1718	Birmingham, Alabama Howard College	1959
1719	Warren, Pennsylvania Trinity Memorial Episcopal Church	1959
1720	Baltimore, Maryland Christ Episcopal Church	1959
1721	Princeton, New Jersey First Presbyterian Church	1959
1722	Cleveland, Ohio—Lakewood St. Peter's Episcopal Church	1959
1723	Nashville, Tennessee Fisk University	1960
1724	Lexington, Kentucky Central Christian Church	1960
1725	Winston-Salem, North Carolina Salem Academy and College—Practice Organ	1959
1726	Berkeley, California University of California—Continuo	1959
1727	Colorado Springs, Colorado Chapel of Our Saviour	1960
1728	Greenville, South Carolina Furman University	1960
1729	Cleveland, Ohio—Parma Holy Trinity Lutheran Church	1960
1730	Lynchburg, Virginia Randolph-Macon Woman's College—Practice Organ	1959
1731	Houston, Texas Zion Lutheran Church	1960
1732*	Springfield, Ohio First Lutheran Church	1961
1733*	Toledo, Ohio Holy Cross Lutheran Church	1961
1734	Blacksburg, Virginia Blacksburg Presbyterian Church	1960
1735	Greenville, South Carolina Furman University—Practice Organ	1960

Job Number	Institution	Date
1736	Cambridge, Massachusetts Massachusetts Institute of Technology—Continuo	1960
1737	Marion, North Carolina First Methodist Church	1961
1738*	Cleveland, Ohio Western Reserve University— Amasa Stone Chapel	1960
1739	Milford, Connecticut Church of Christ, Congregational	1961
1740	Cleveland, Ohio Fairmount Presbyterian Church Chapel	1961
1741	Cleveland, Ohio—Shaker Heights First Unitarian Church of Cleveland	1960
1742	Collegeville, Minnesota St. John's Abbey	1961

It is difficult to determine exactly where to end the listing of the work of Walter Holtkamp. By late 1961 his son was playing an important role in the firm in partnership with Walter Holtkamp. However, it is clear that, while Holtkamp, Sr. did continue to provide leadership until his death on 11 February 1962, the organ for St. John's Abbey was his last major work.

*First instruments designed, constructed and tonally finished under supervision of Walter Holtkamp, Jr.

Sources Cited

A. Works in Print

Barnes, William H. *The Contemporary American Organ*, 6th ed. New York: J. Fischer & Bro., 1956.

Blanton, Joseph. *The Organ in Church Design*. Albany, Texas: Venture Press, 1957.

Blodgett, Walter. *Notes for Inaugural Concert, McMyler Memorial Organ*. Cleveland: Cleveland Museum of Art, 1971.

Bullis, Carleton H. "New Rueckpositiv on Cleveland Organ Is First in America." *The Diapason* 25 (December 1933) p. 11.

Fesperman, John. *Two Essays on Organ Design*. Raleigh: Sunbury Press, 1975.

Holtkamp, Walter. "An Organ to See and Hear." *The American Organist* 18 (July 1934) pp. 269–72.

_____. "Organ Music and Organ Architecture." *Architecture*, June 1934, pp. 355–56, 372.

_____. "Present-Day Trends in Organ Building." *Proceedings of the Music Teachers National Association* (Cleveland, 1940). pp. 395–403.

_____. "The Modern Organ." *American Lutheran* 16 (March 1933) pp. 10–13.

Nye, Eugene M. "Walter Holtkamp—A Master Organ Builder." *The Organ* 51 (October 1971) pp. 66–78.

Ochse, Orpha. *The History of the Organ in the United States*. Bloomington: Indiana University Press, 1975.

Phelps, Lawrence I. *A Short History of the Organ Revival*. St. Louis: Concordia Publishing House, 1967.

Thompson, Arthur J. "Some Reflections on Organ Ensemble." *The Diapason* 18 (March 1927) p. 40.

Webber, F. R. "A Holtkamp Story." *The Diapason* 53 (April 1962) pp. 28–29.

B. **Other Sources**

Blodgett, Walter, Cleveland Museum of Art, Cleveland, Ohio. Interview, June 18, 1973.

———. Cleveland, to John Ferguson. 23 October 1974.

Bonnet, Joseph. New York, to Walter Holtkamp. 5 March 1942.

Cleveland, Ohio. Holtkamp Organ Company. Incomplete Manuscript for a Book on Organ Building. Walter Holtkamp, Sr.

Flentrop, Dick. Zaadam, Netherlands, to John Ferguson. 7 April 1978.

Fountain, Grigg. Evanston, to John Ferguson. 15 July 1975.

Holtkamp, Walter. Address to the Cleveland Chapter American Guild of Organists, 1932. Text in Holtkamp archives.

———. "My Philosophy of Organ Building." Paper presented to the annual meeting of the Chicago Chapter American Guild of Organists, 22 May 1939. Text in Holtkamp archives.

———. Cleveland, to the Very Reverend Ignatius Wagner. 5 March 1932 and 30 March 1932.

Holktamp, Walter, Jr. Holtkamp Organ Company, Cleveland. Interviews, 21 April 1975, 6 May 1975, and 10 July 1975.

McManis, Charles. Kansas City, Kansas, to John Ferguson. 10 August 1975.

Noss, Luther. New Haven, Connecticut, to John Ferguson. 20 February 1978.

Poister, Arthur. Kent, Ohio. Interview, 9 November 1973.

Quimby, Arthur. Plainfield, New Hampshire, to John Ferguson. 18 July 1975.

Raver, Leonard. New York, to John Ferguson.

Schweitzer, Albert. Gunsbach, Alsace, to Walter Holtkamp. 22 May 1934.

Sittler, Joseph. "A Biographical Sketch of Walter Holtkamp's Evolving Tonal Philosophy." Holtkamp archives.

Smith, Martha. Cambridge, Massachusetts, to Walter Holtkamp, Jr. 25 May 1975.

Videro, Finn. Copenhagen, Denmark, to John Ferguson. 5 April 1978.